Techniques for Casual Clothes

from *Threads*

Techniques
for
Casual
Clothes

from *Threads*

The Taunton Press

Cover photo by Yvonne Taylor

BOOKS & VIDEOS

for fellow enthusiasts

First printing: January 1994
Second printing: January 1995
Printed in the United States of America

A THREADS Book

THREADS® is a trademark of The Taunton Press, Inc.,
registered in the U.S. Patent and Trademark Office.

The Taunton Press
63 South Main Street
Box 5506
Newtown, CT 06470-5506

Library of Congress Cataloging-in-Publication Data

Techniques for casual clothes from Threads.
     p. cm.
   "A Threads book."
   Includes index.
   ISBN 1-56158-071-6
    1. Sport clothes. 2. Sewing. 3. Tailoring.
TT649.T37   1994   93-32087
646.4 — dc20   CIP

Contents

Introduction

omfortable, casual clothes—colorful, loose shirts, a knock-around coat, a favorite vest—these are what we wear most of the time. There's no better reason to sew than to make such personalized favorites.

And here is a selection of articles from *Threads* magazine that makes creating clothes as much fun as wearing them. Whether you stencil cowboy hats all over a plain bowling shirt, add your favorite embroidery to a warm, colorful melton coat, or draft a pattern for a pair of jeans that even Calvin Klein would envy, *Threads* offers you the how-to information you need for success.

Amy T. Yanagi, editor

Straight Line Design

Shape squares with tabs, loops, and buttons

by Suzen Hahn

the simplest concept in design is the straight line. As a garment designer, one of my biggest challenges is bringing together the straight line and fabric, a medium in which hard, straight edges are difficult to attain. I constantly manipulate the straight line to find new shapes and styles.

My clothing (which I market under the name Su-Zen) is based on simple geometric shapes: rectangles, squares, and trapezoids. I let the human form shape the clothing, instead of shaping the body with clothes.

To add interest and detail to the basic garments, I combine fabrics in subtle ways with trims and use unusual buttons and button loops. Pleats or tabs of fabric add unexpected, eye-catching folds down the center of a garment. Sometimes pockets are where no one expects them—below the knees on a dress, for instance.

Every fabric I use must have "personality," a subtle woven texture, nice colors, a good hand. If a fabric doesn't say something on its own, it won't mean anything after you sew it into a garment. I put fabrics together not by matching colors, but by combining patterns and colors that complement each other. At Su-Zen, we work mostly with cotton, rayon, and linen, and have developed an individual and appealing way of expressing ourselves through textiles and clothing.

On pp. 12 and 13, you'll find instructions for drafting a simple jacket or top. Combine that with some of the embellishments below, and experiment to find your own style.

Simple additions for details

To shape or finish a garment, we often sew a *tab*, a square or rectangle of contrasting fabric, onto the basic shape. These can be pure-

Cropped top, reversible jacket, jacket with co-ordinating trim: all were made from the same basic pattern. The secret is in the detail and trim. The pattern draft is on p. 13; author Suzen Hahn gives hints for inventive tricks and trims. (Photo by Yvonne Taylor)

ly decorative, but they also hold elastic or fabric button loops and pleats, or form reinforcements under buttons. Usually the contrasting fabric has been used in the garment as edging, in-seam pockets, or facings. Sometimes the tabs are embellished with contrasting stitching or binding.

To make a tab, measure the size you need and add ½ in. all around. Press the ½ in. under, then pin the tab down and sew to the garment as close to the edge as possible, making sure the corners stay tucked under. You can also stitch across the tab in an X to reinforce it, as shown in the top drawing on p. 10.

Instead of making buttonholes, we use button loops. You can make fabric loops out of contrasting or matching fabric, or from elastic. Sew them in a facing seam, or use a tab to secure the loose ends. Narrow, flat elastic is available from Active Trimming Co., 250 W. 34th St., New York, NY 10018; (212) 921-7114 (minimum order: 288 yd. spool, $15.50). Round elastic will eventually pull out of a seam.

Placing loop elastic in a seam is a little bit tricky at first. The drawing at center left on p. 10 shows how to measure the elastic to length and presew the loops. To sew a loop into a facing seam, mark loop placement. Then lay the facing on the garment, right sides together, with the garment on the bottom. Put a pin through both pieces at the loop mark. Sew up to the pin, then slip the loop under the facing with the cut ends even with the edges of the fabric, as shown in the lower left drawing on p. 10. Butt the loop against the pin and sew over the pin by turning the handwheel to avoid hitting it. After stitching over the loop, remove the pin and backstitch twice to secure.

For elastic loops with a tab, the process is similar. Cut out your tab, press the ½-in. seam allowance under, and place it ⅛ in. to ¼ in. away from the garment edge. Secure the tab with pins and tuck ½ in. of the loop ends under the tab (see the drawing at lower right, p. 10). To secure, we usually stitch

the loop side of the tab at least twice. Sometimes we sew a button on top of the tab for a kind of double-breasted look. We sometimes add a tab under the corresponding buttons. This is an attractive way to add strength to the stress point where the button is sewn.

Attach fabric loops to your garments in the same way as the elastic loops. They look especially good with large buttons, and on heavy garments like jackets and coats. The simplest kind of fabric loop to make is one that is folded flat and top-stitched, as shown in the drawing at center right, p. 10. It can be cut on the straight grain or on the bias. Size your loop in proportion to your button. Cut a fabric strip four times the finished width, and place the right side of the fabric face down on the ironing board. Fold the sides in equally to meet at the center. Press flat, and then fold in half and press again. Stitch as close as possible to the edge. To determine how long to cut your loops, measure your button diameter, subtract ⅟₁₆ in., then double; add seam allowance to both ends. For a ½-in. button you would need a 1⅞ in. loop.

Sometimes when a garment is quite plain in cut, we make it more "Su-zen" by adding some fun buttons. We choose buttons that are made from natural materials like shells, horn, or nuts. Sometimes they are handmade, vintage, or from exotic places. Finding unusual buttons takes a bit of hunting in thrift shops, antique or specialty stores, or from mail-order sources. I have found that nothing makes a person happier than these special touches, and when people talk to me about our clothes, the first thing they say is "...and you always have those great buttons," or "Where do you get your buttons?" One of my favorite sources is Renaissance Buttons (826 W. Armitage, Chicago, IL 60622; 312-883-9508).

Buttons added at or near the neckline, either with or without a tab, can often take the place of a necklace.

We often use buttons to reshape a garment. To narrow a sleeve or hem, fold in the amount of fabric that you want to eliminate, pin, then sew your buttons on through all thicknesses.

Places for pockets

Making pockets is easy, and you can put them in more places than you might think. We add odd-sized pockets in unexpected places. We use them in sizes from 1½-in. square to ones that almost cover the back of a jacket.

Use pockets with a sense of humor, but make sure to keep the balance of the whole garment in mind when thinking about proportion and placement. Try to place pockets and buttons only after the whole body of the garment is put together. Take a big scrap of the fabric with which you are working, and fold it to the approximate size you want to use. Then try on the garment or put it on a mannequin, and with the help of a mirror, see what looks good to your eye. Placing a pocket on something when it is flat on a table can be very deceiving. What looks like the right placement off the body, especially for shirts, can end up being under your arm when you try it on.

For a straight-edged patch pocket, measure the length and width you need and plot them on paper. Add seam allowances to the bottom and both sides. To the top, add the amount you want to turn down (our standard pocket hem is 1 in.) plus ⅜ in. to turn under. To make a shaped patch pocket, draw your shape and then use the same formula as for a straight pocket.

There are some easy variations you can use with this basic pocket idea. Instead of a hem at the top of the pocket, you can eliminate all allowance at the top and finish with a contrasting bias. To insert a loop in the top of your pocket so you can close it with a button, finish the pocket with a facing. Decide on the facing width, then add a seam allowance to one side and ⅜ in. to the other. Sew the facing and pocket together, turn right side out, and sew the facing down, turning under the ⅜ in. If you want your pocket to be functional, think about what you need it for, and make sure it is big enough; if you want pockets that you can slip your hands into, make sure they are wide enough for your hand.

Bias bindings for necklines

At Su-zen, we do a lot of open necklines without collars. Finishing necklines with facings can be a time-consuming process; edging with bias is faster and neater looking. A bias trim from contrasting fabric loses nothing aesthetically.

One way to use bias binding is to sew it so it shows on both sides of the garment. When sewing bias, the rule is to pull the

Illustrations by Suzen Hahn

Tabs and loops

Use these little holders for everything from button loops to garment tabs.

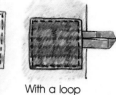

Press edges under ½ in., keeping corners hidden.

Stitched with an X

Holding a pleat

With a loop and buttons

With fabric loop

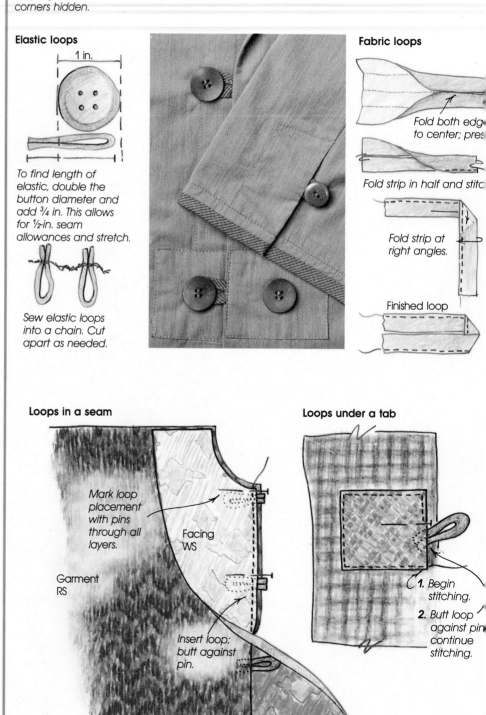

Elastic loops

1 in.

To find length of elastic, double the button diameter and add ¾ in. This allows for ½-in. seam allowances and stretch.

Sew elastic loops into a chain. Cut apart as needed.

Fabric loops

Fold both edge to center; pres

Fold strip in half and stitc

Fold strip at right angles.

Finished loop

Loops in a seam

Mark loop placement with pins through all layers.

Facing WS

Garment RS

Insert loop; butt against pin.

Loops under a tab

1. Begin stitching.

2. Butt loop against pin continue stitching.

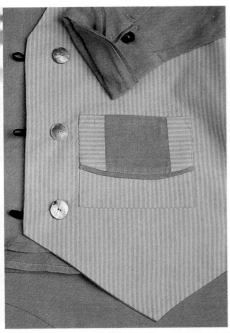

This is a variation of the simple patch pocket. The rectangular pocket has a shaped facing, turned to the outside, with contrasting trim. Note the bias strip in the facing's bottom hem.

Bias edging provides a clean, attractive neckline finish, whether covering both inner and outer edges of the garment, or turned to one side. The contrast in pattern and texture, as in the pocket, changes a simple garment into a designer original. Contrasting facings and vegetable ivory buttons complement the look.

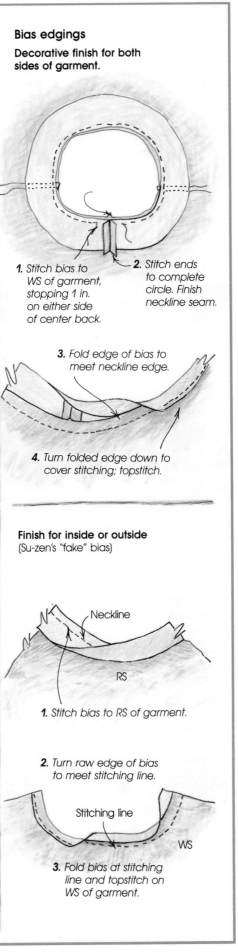

Bias edgings
Decorative finish for both sides of garment.

1. Stitch bias to WS of garment, stopping 1 in. on either side of center back.

2. Stitch ends to complete circle. Finish neckline seam.

3. Fold edge of bias to meet neckline edge.

4. Turn folded edge down to cover stitching; topstitch.

Finish for inside or outside
(Su-zen's "fake" bias)

Neckline

RS

1. Stitch bias to RS of garment.

2. Turn raw edge of bias to meet stitching line.

Stitching line

WS

3. Fold bias at stitching line and topstitch on WS of garment.

bias on a curve, and pull the garment on a straight seam. In the case of the neckline, you will be keeping the garment taut when sewing the center front and back, and stretching the bias everywhere else.

For a two-sided bias, cut a strip of bias fabric four times the desired finished width, and at least long enough to reach all the way around the neckline, plus a ¾-in. seam allowance. Trim the ends of the bias square. Mark the center back of your garment with a notch. Then turn the garment wrong side out, and place the bias strip right side down on it, making sure the raw edges are even. Leaving ⅜ in. of the bias strip free for a seam allowance at the center back, pin the bias to the garment. Start stitching about 1 in. from the center back pin (drawing at top, near left), and continue around to within 1 in. of the center back. Break the stitching, and mark where the two ends of the bias will meet the center-back line. Then sew the bias ends together with a ½-in. seam allowance, trimming off any excess. Finish sewing the neck seam, finger pressing the seam open.

Turn the garment right side out, and make two folds in the bias strip: one to bring the raw edge of the bias to meet the raw neck edge, and the second bringing the folded edge just to cover the stitching as shown at left. Pin in place or hold by hand and topstitch on the right side as close to the edge as possible. Be careful not to pull the bias, or it will pucker.

We call a bias that finishes only one side or one that finishes off a neckline with a collar a "fake bias," although it is just as much a bias as the other method. For this technique (bottom drawings, left), add an extra seam allowance to your pattern, and cut your bias three times the finished trim width. Start with the garment right side out. Place the bias right side down and stitch as for the two-sided bias. Turn the garment wrong side up, folding the bias over so that the seam you just made becomes the neck edge. Now fold the bias in half so that the raw edge just meets the stitching line. From the wrong side of the garment, topstitch the bias as close to the folded edge as you can. If you have a collar, make sure you keep it out of the way, so you don't topstitch over it.

We also use this method for sleeve and bottom hems. It gives a nicer finish than a rolled hem and can also be done in a contrasting fabric. The bias can finish to the outside if a binding on both sides would look too bulky. ⇨

Suzen Hahn is a clothing designer based in Chicago, IL. Her lines are shown regularly in New York and sold in retail stores across the country.

Basic draft; basic top

by Suzen Hahn

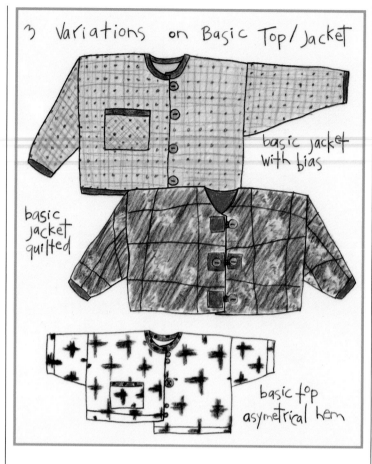

3 Variations on Basic Top/Jacket

basic jacket with bias

basic jacket quilted

basic top asymetrical hem

Before I went to design school, I felt frustrated by not knowing how to make even the simplest patterns. When a friend made me a fitted camisole by drawing the measurements directly onto the fabric, I discovered that patternmaking was not the rocket science that everyone said it was. There are many things you can do with no pattern at all, just a few measurements, a piece of paper, and a pencil.

I begin by making a thumbnail sketch of the garment that includes all seams and details (see the sketches at right). By comparing the proportions of the drawn garment to my own measurements, I establish the basic garment dimensions (length, width, and size of front and back neckline). Then I draft the pattern.

Taking pencil in hand

Drafting is simply drawing a pattern on paper using given measurements. I use a commercial marker paper with marks at 1-in. intervals, which makes drafting square shapes very quick. Many fabric stores sell this paper by the yard. Brown kraft paper or white butcher paper works well, too. Try to find paper at least 45 in. wide. You will need a minimum of three yards to draft the basic top.

Your other supplies will include a good metal ruler 45 in. to 60 in. long, an L square, a french curve, and a clear plastic ruler 2 in. wide by 18 in. long. If you don't have all of these, the most versatile tool is the clear plastic ruler.

The pattern draft on the facing page will give you the pattern for the basic top or jacket sketched above. These variations are only a few of the many you can make once you've drafted the basic pattern.

The same steps apply to drafting all the major pieces of this pattern. First, you will establish the *center*, either of the body (center front and back) or of the pattern piece itself (sleeve). All subsequent lines are drawn from this center reference line.

After drafting one main pattern piece, in this case the right front, many lines are simply copied from it to form the other pieces. When copying, mark the corners with short lines and curves with dashed lines, then connect the marks with the ruler or french curve. This avoids the wavy lines which sometimes result from trying to trace along the edge of another paper.

It's easy to get a football-shaped neckline, with points at both ends, instead of a nice oval. You can avoid this by making a very gentle curve, and, at the shoulder and center of the neckline, by keeping at least ½ in. in a straight line. The easiest way to do this is to draw a ½-in. line perpendicular to shoulder and center lines, then connect it with your curve (see the top left drawing opposite). I

draw curved lines freehand first, then use the french curve to make a clean, solid line.

Pattern parts like the front facing extension and the sleeve hem that need to be mirror images of the pattern itself are drafted in a special way. Keep the pattern paper uncut along the edge connecting the two parts, and fold it under the pattern after you have cut out the main piece, as shown at top right, opposite. Then you can copy as much of the pattern as you need for the extension, resulting in a perfect fit.

The last steps in drafting are to label each piece, mark the grainline, and add a ½-in. seam allowance to each seam. Labels include the body part (sleeve, front) and how many to cut. This pattern is cut completely on the lengthwise grain, so you mark the grainline by putting arrow tips near the ends of the center lines, as shown in the drawings on the facing page. Seam allowances are

included in the pieces copied from the right front, but you will need to add them to the left front and sleeve patterns.

Putting it all together

Begin assembling your basic top by sewing the shoulder seams. Sew the side seams from the hem toward the shoulder, leaving 12½ in. from the shoulder open for setting the sleeve. A good way to finish seams is to serge them, then turn them to one side and topstitch on the right side to hold them down.

Sew and finish the sleeve seam, and either hem the sleeve or finish it with bias binding. Matching the center of the sleeve with the shoulder seam, set the sleeve into the armhole.

Clean finish (see *Threads*, No. 36, pp. 16 and 18) the left front extension. Then turn the extension under on the fold line (1½ in. from CF) and stitch it in place. Now is the time to try on the basic top and mark the placement of button loops on the right front. You can space them evenly down the front, or you can group them. Think about using buttons of different sizes or colors to add interest.

Sew the elastic loops under the right front facing, and sew on the buttons. Bind the neck with bias binding, and hem; your basic top is finished.

Using any of the techniques described earlier, you can make your garment this simple or more detailed with pockets, tabs, or extra buttons. You can change the neckline. You can cut each piece double and make your garment quilted or reversible. Remember, this is a *basic* top. As you begin to understand how patternmaking works, you can easily make simple adjustments like a shaped hemline, a yoke, or a more fitted shoulder line. For me, this patternmaking format creates an empty canvas on which I can begin working. □

An easy basic-top draft

Measurements are based on Su-Zen's one-size sloper and include substantial design ease. Alter the measurements to suit your taste.

Drafting the right front (RF)

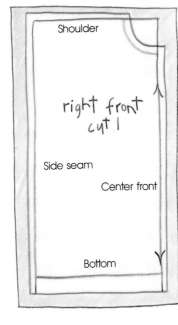

1. Draw **center-front** (CF) line, 30 in. long.

2. From top of CF, draw a perpendicular **shoulder** line, 14 in. long.

3. From end of shoulder, draw a perpendicular **side seam**, 28 in. long.

4. Mark CF line 28 in. down from shoulder and draw **bottom** line from end of side seam to mark on CF.

5. Make **front neckline:** Mark CF and shoulder 4 in. from their intersection. Keeping ½ in. at either end straight, draw neckline curve.

6. Add ½-in. seam allowances and a 2-in. hem; label and cut out.

Using RF to draft left front (LF)

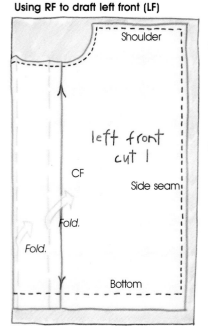

1. Draw CF line 5 in. from left edge of paper. Place RF face down on LF, matching CF lines. Copy RF.

2. Cut out LF, except CF and neck edge, then fold under ½ in. on front extension edge. Fold again 1½ in. from CF. Cut neckline through all thicknesses, forming shaped **facing**.

Drafting the back from the RF

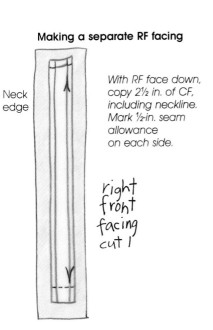

1. Draw a **center-back** (CB) line, 30 in. long. Place RF on back, matching CF to CB. Copy RF, including neckline.

2. Make **back neckline** by marking CB 1½ in. from top. Starting at front neckline mark on shoulder line, and keeping the first ¾ in. straight, draw back neckline curve.

3. Cut out completed half of pattern only. Do not cut on CB. Fold on CB, and copy for second half.

Making a separate RF facing

With RF face down, copy 2½ in. of CF, including neckline. Mark ½-in. seam allowance on each side.

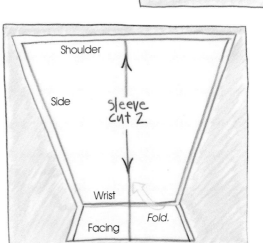

Sleeve drafting

1. Draw a 20-in. **center** line.

2. Draw 25-in. **shoulder** line at top and 11-in. **wrist** line, 16 in. to 18 in. below shoulder.

3. Connect ends of shoulder and wrist lines.

4. Add seam allowances to shoulder and sides. Cut out, leaving 4-in. extension at bottom. Fold under on wrist line and cut shaped **facing** along side lines.

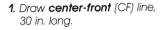

Photo by Yvonne Taylor

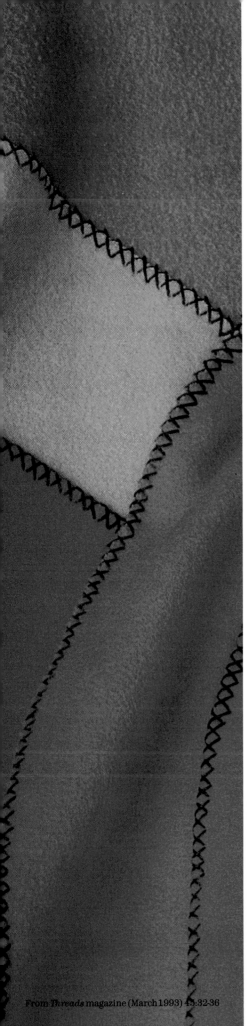

Marvelous Melton

Stable fabric and simple lapped seams free you to concentrate on color

by Linda Faiola

Want to make a great winter coat? If you're willing to sacrifice the bulky seams and layers of lining and interfacing used in traditional coat construction, warm and colorful melton wool is an ideal choice of fabric. Like coat-weight leather, melton is thick, and difficult to tailor. But if you treat melton like leather, lapping the seams and applying a decorative stitch on the surface, making a coat becomes an enjoyable project rather than a chore.

Starting with a basic pattern that you may already have, you can eliminate hems and facings, and instead concentrate on color. You can cut up the pattern into simple or complicated shapes that would be difficult to stitch with traditional seams, and use the new shapes to add blocks of color or interesting design lines. Here's how to have some fun with melton, by hand or machine.

Fabric information

Melton cloth is first woven into yardage and then compressed, or felted, to create the characteristic thick, nappy texture.

Best known as the fabric in a Navy pea coat, melton is now available to the home sewer in a wide range of colors in both all wool and wool blends. If your local store doesn't carry melton, you can order it by mail in a selection of up to 20 colors from $14.99 to $27.99 per yard from Vogue Fabrics (718 Main St., Evanston, IL 60202; 708-864-9600, ask for Liz; please indicate color preferences for complimentary swatching service).

Choosing and testing a pattern

I recommend a jacket, coat, or vest pattern with simple lines. Avoid fitted, set-in sleeves, gathers, and other complicated construction details, because they will be hard to work in thick melton. A pattern with a slight amount of ease at the back shoulder line or a curved princess seam over the bustline is fine.

Large patch pockets, either curved or square, can add attractive design lines to a basic coat. Even if your pattern doesn't have pockets, they're easy to add. You can also apply a standard in-seam pocket, using a thin, tightly woven fabric for one or both layers to reduce bulk. ⇨

Lap and stitch a melton jacket with sweeps of color and bits of embroidered detail. The soft, felted woven wool fabric doesn't ravel, which eliminates the need for interfacings and lining and simplifies garment construction.

From *Threads* magazine (March 1993) 45:32-36

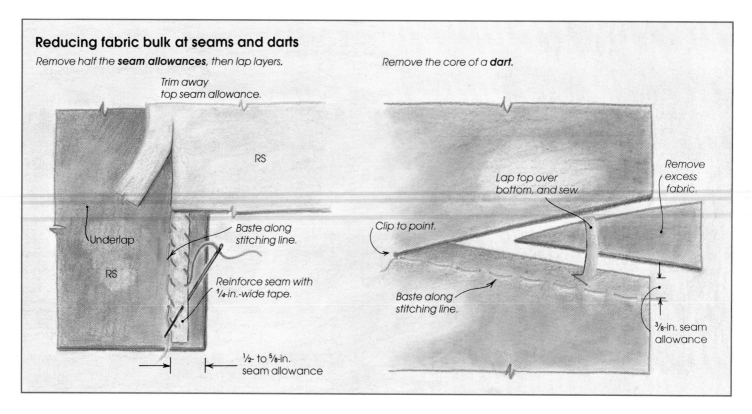

Reducing fabric bulk at seams and darts

*Remove half the **seam allowances**, then lap layers.*

*Remove the core of a **dart**.*

Trim away
top seam allowance.

RS

Underlap

RS

Baste along
stitching line.

Reinforce seam with
¼-in.-wide tape.

½- to ⅝-in.
seam allowance

Lap top over
bottom, and sew.

Clip to point.

Baste along
stitching line.

Remove
excess
fabric.

⅜-in. seam
allowance

If you haven't sewed the pattern before, first make a test garment in muslin from the main body and sleeve pieces. All my coats are single layers of fabric, so sleeves and hems cannot be lengthened once the pieces are cut. Pay special attention to the following areas:

Hemline—Turn up the hem to your desired finished length. Don't feel constrained by the hemline shown on the pattern; you can adjust it to be straight, curved, or angled, or even cut the pattern fuller at the bottom, as I've done for the coat on the cover. Don't be afraid to experiment. That's the reason for a test garment. Trim the excess as one piece, and use it to adjust the pattern.

Sleeve length—The sleeve hem is as flexible as the hemline. Pin or baste it to the desired finished length.

Neckline—Patterns usually have a ⅝-in. seam allowance at the neckline. When you try on the muslin and look at the neckline without a collar or a facing, you can decide where you want the neckline to finish. A collarless garment needs no seam allowance at the neck, while one with a collar needs a ¼-in. seam allowance, which you can add after you determine the correct neckline placement. Don't cut the seam allowance away all at once. Trim a little at a time, checking the neckline after each trim, because the neckline might look better without taking away the entire ⅝ in. For a too-low

back neckline, you might trim away ⅝ in. at the center front and only ¼ in. at the center back. When you're happy with the neckline, add a ¼-in. seam allowance, if needed, for attaching a collar.

Save the trimmings to use as guides when correcting the stitching lines on the pattern. Just pin each muslin scrap to the appropriate pattern and redraw the seamlines and cutting lines.

Reducing the bulk at seams

At each seam, decide which edge you want to lap on top. The under piece keeps its seam allowance, while that of the top piece is trimmed away (as shown in the drawing above).

The width of the seam allowance varies depending on location and seam shape. Allow a ½- to ⅝-in. seam allowance for straight seams and ⅜ in. for curves and darts. If the garment has a collar, leave only a ¼-in. seam allowance on the neckline edge of the garment, lap the collar onto the neckline, and sew this narrow seam allowance securely.

Melton is too thick for a traditional folded dart, so I trim and lap darts the same way I do the seams. Decide which way you want each dart to lap: For a horizontal bustline dart, I suggest lapping the top stitching line over the bottom for smoothness. Leave a ⅜-in. seam allowance on the side of the dart that will lap underneath, and cut along the stitching line that will lay on top, removing the center of the dart (see the drawing above). Lap, baste, and sew by hand or machine.

Creating new seams

Adding new seams to make blocks of color or interesting shapes is a creative way to personalize your garment. Draw on the muslin first to decide where to make the additional cuts. Avoid too many seams meeting in the same place, which results in a bulky meeting point. Draw the new stitching lines smoothly, for curved and straight lines.

To transfer the additional seamlines and any corrected stitching lines to the pattern, you must first take the muslin apart and press the pieces flat. You can place the muslin over the pattern piece and use a tracing wheel to transfer the new and corrected stitching lines to the pattern. Or you can place a transparent pattern over the muslin piece and trace the new and corrected stitching lines from the muslin to the pattern. This technique of lap and stitch depends upon the pieces fitting together like a jigsaw puzzle. Pattern pieces must be accurate, so double-check all corresponding stitching lines to make sure that they're the same length.

Draw a grainline on each new piece before separating it from the original garment section. If you add new long seams, mark one or two spots along the length of each side as notches to help in matching the seams during assembly. After separating the pieces, decide which way they will lap, and then add the appropriate seam allowances to one side. For example, if the new front side seam is going to lap onto the back side seam, then add no

Stitching a melton coat by hand or machine

I enjoy handsewing, so the idea of making a garment totally by hand appeals to me. Embroidering seams with a heavy thread, as shown at right, goes much more quickly than you might think. You can achieve a similar embroidered effect by stitching the seams with a decorative or overlock machine stitch.

Curves and shaped pieces are easier to assemble by hand. It can be tricky to maneuver a large section, such as the coat back, through a sewing machine while following a curved shape. If you assemble your coat by machine, stay with simpler shapes, especially for a first project.

Taping for support—Before assembling the pieces, I recommend taping seams that support a lot of weight, such as the neck, shoulder seams, and armholes, to add stability and prevent stretching. I use a ¼-in. cotton tape (see the drawing on the facing page) called sailors' tape, available from Oregon Tailor Supply (2123 S.E. Division St., PO Box 42284, Portland, OR 97242; 503-232-6191). Wash and dry the tape to preshrink. Measure the length of the seam on the pattern and cut a piece of tape, adding an inch for turning the ends under. Pin the tape to the right side of the underlapping seam allowance, and sew it in place by whipping along both edges. The tape will not show after stitching, since it will be sandwiched between the layers of melton.

If your coat has a collar, place the supporting tape for the neckline on the right side, close to the neck edge. For a collarless neckline, sew a ¼-in. grosgrain ribbon, in a coordinating color, on the inside of the garment. Coax the tape or ribbon into a curve using steam: hold one end of the tape with the point of a steam iron, then curve and press along the length. They won't curve a lot, but some shape will help in fitting to the neckline.

Hand stitching a coat

If your sewing skills include embroidery, patchwork, or appliqué, you'll love sewing this coat by hand. I use cross stitch, because it gives the look of lacing on leather. It's also easy to decorate the coat with appliqué, since melton doesn't ravel.

Marking seamlines—After cutting the fabric pieces and thread-marking all the notches, I baste along the seamlines on the sides with the seam allowances. I draw

Cross stitching a lapped seam by hand

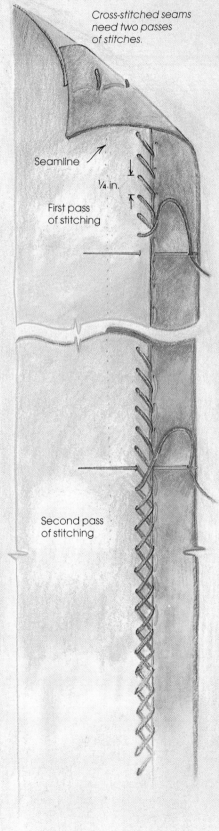

Cross-stitched seams need two passes of stitches.

Seamline

¼ in.

First pass of stitching

Second pass of stitching

the seamline on the wrong side of the fabric with a ruler and chalk, then baste along the chalk line so that the basting is visible on the right side. This basting line provides a guide for tape placement and makes it easy to lap accurately onto the stitching line. If you prefer, you can mark with chalk on the right side, then pin-baste.

Melton is dense and edge threads don't ravel, but to prevent fraying, I still like to overcast the edges by hand with one strand of a matching sewing thread before beginning to lap the pieces. Don't worry about these stitches showing, because they disappear after you topstitch with the thicker thread.

Choosing a thread and needle—I prefer to cross stitch the seams on my coats with a single or double strand of silk buttonhole twist, which is heavier than typical sewing thread, because it's glossy and shows up well. A variety of silk threads is available from Oregon Tailor Supply including heavyweight tailors' silk twist in 10 menswear colors (such as black, brown, white, gray, khaki), the discontinued Belding silk twist in 28 colors, and Gütermann silk topstitching thread (slightly lighter than buttonhole twist) in 25 colors.

You can also sew with a double strand of polyester buttonhole twist, available at most fabric stores, or three to six strands of cotton embroidery floss, or even a single strand of a fine yarn, such as a fingering-weight silk yarn. Try a variety of threads on swatches of your fabric before deciding which thread you want to use.

I like the way black cross stitching shows up on bright or deep colors, but it's fun to experiment with other colors. For a variegated effect, choose several bright or coordinating thread colors, and sew with a needleful of each, changing colors each time you fill your needle.

I find the cross stitching easiest to sew with a small needle, such as a No. 5 embroidery/crewel needle. Experiment to find a needle that is comfortable for you.

Waxing a doubled strand of thread makes sewing easier, because the doubled thread then handles like a single thread. Wax can mark the fabric, though, so run your fingers along the waxed thread to remove excess, or take a few stitches through a cloth scrap, after threading the needle but before knotting the thread. ⇨

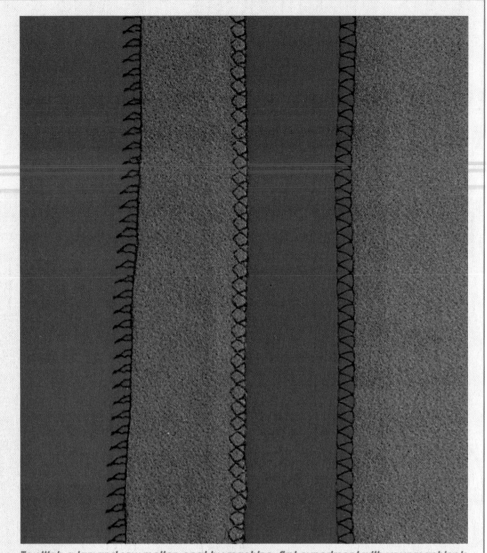

To stitch a lap-and-sew melton coat by machine, first experiment with your machine's stitches. These samples, sewn on a Pfaff 1473, use a cotton/poly button-and-carpet thread in the needle (size 18), and regular sewing thread in the bobbin. At left, an edge-binding stitch resembles the hand buttonhole stitch; at center is a closed overlock stitch; and at right is a pullover stitch.

The ends of the overcasting thread hide easily in the thickness of the wool. Run the needle into the layer.

Cross stitching is fast and easy. Overlap the seam edges, pin every few inches, and sew one pass, hiding the knot between the layers. On the second pass, cross each stitch, reinforcing the end stitches by sewing them twice.

After sewing, avoid cutting through the threads of the hand stitching. Unlike machine stitching, which locks itself, the cut cross stitches unravel easily.

Stitching by machine

If you decide to assemble your jacket or coat by machine, I recommend lapping and basting the seams with a long machine stitch instead of basting along the underlap seamline. Then you can maneuver the seam through the machine without worrying about shifting.

A heavier thread is more visible for machine stitching, as well as for hand stitching. Try silk or polyester buttonhole twist thread, a topstitching thread, or a button-and-carpet thread in the needle, and use regular sewing thread in the bobbin. You'll probably need to loosen the upper thread tension to produce a balanced stitch. The swatches above show several stitch options. What you use depends on the stitches available on your machine and the effect that you want. Experiment with stitches on swatches of your fabric before making a decision. —L.F.

seam allowance to the front side seam, and add a ½-in. seam allowance to the back side seam.

General pattern changes

On my coats, I usually eliminate hems and facings, finishing the nonraveling raw edges with the type of stitching I used for the seams. There is one exception: I sometimes leave a 1½-in.-wide facing at the center fronts to turn back and hand-sew, especially when I plan to insert a front zipper. The extra fabric adds stability to a front opening that doesn't overlap.

Other closures that work well include buttons with hand-worked buttonholes, buttons with loops of thread or braid, and frog fasteners. None of these require a front facing.

Sometimes I add a facing to a collar that needs the extra body. Cut a facing identical to the collar, and sew them, wrong sides together, along the outer edge. After reinforcing the neckline of the coat with ¼-in. tape, as described on p. 17, lap the collar over the coat neckline, baste in place, and sew. Handsew the facing inside. Last, finish the front collar edges.

Because of the thickness of melton fabric, cutting a pattern on the fold is inaccurate. Instead, make a full pattern by attaching another piece of paper and drawing the complete garment section, and then cut it out on a single layer of fabric. Another solution is to use the pattern as is. Mark the fabric fold line with basting. Open the fabric and match the pattern fold line to the basting. Cut the pattern, without cutting along the fold/baste line. Then flip the pattern over onto the other side of the basted line, and finish cutting.

For any garment area, such as a dart or collar, that requires you to adapt your pattern, experiment with a swatch of fabric or paper first to test the results.

Marking the fabric

When you're using lapped seams, you cannot cut out, cut in, or clip to mark the location of notches and other pattern sewing symbols. Instead, you should use thread markings such as tailors' tacks (see *Threads*, No. 45, p. 16) to note symbols, placing the thread marks at the stitching line on the pattern. Choose your method of assembly from the instructions on p. 17, and you're on your way to an enjoyable winter coat. □

Linda Faiola is a professional pattern maker and machine knitter who teaches classes in quilting, handknitting, and pattern making at the Cambridge Center for Adult Education in Cambridge, MA.

Making Great Strides

How to put a perfect pleat into a straight skirt

by Linda Faiola

love to observe the way people dress. A sight that amuses me is a woman wearing athletic shoes with a straight-skirted business suit. She can walk with sure short steps to and from work, but that last step onto the commuter train is a difficult maneuver. She'd be more comfortable with a pleat or vent in the skirt.

I'm going to share some patternmaking techniques for adding the perfect pleat, inverted pleat, or vent to a straight or flared skirt pattern (photo at left). You can apply the same techniques that help the skirt and pleat hang so well to pleats in blouses and coats. I'll also explain how to hem the pleat or vent so that the hem is smooth and the underlay never peeks out from under the hem.

The fabric for the body of a plain pleat or a vent is cut as part of the skirt; the difference between the two is that the underlay of a pleat is sewn closed while a vent is an open slit. An inverted pleat, also called a box pleat, requires you to cut a separate underlay from additional fabric. I prefer a vent to either type of pleat for the back of a skirt because the vent

The trick to getting a vent or a pleat to hang just right is in placing the center front or back offgrain just before adding the pleat allowance. Linda Faiola turned the underlay of the front inverted pleat, in the skirt shown at left, into a design element. The pieced underlay reveals chevrons when the pleat opens.

wears better when it's sat upon and it is less bulky. Either pleat is good-looking when placed in the skirt front.

Patternmaking is not an exact science, so there is no absolute amount of change that works every time. I strongly recommend that you make a muslin (test garment) to check out the pleat modifications before working with the real fabric; the experts do. When you get the results you want, use the pattern again and again.

An offgrain center

It can be difficult to fit a straight skirt so that it hangs well, even on a flawless body. A straight skirt's seams are all parallel to the lengthwise grain, except for the curving side seams from waist to hip. The fabric starts moving outward from the waist to the hip and it *wants to keep going*, not drop straight down from the hip. The result is a skirt that pulls in below the hip and appears to cling to the body, and a pleat or vent that gaps open even if the wearer is standing.

If you add width at the center back or front to take the seam offgrain, as shown in the drawing at near right, the extra fabric allows the seam to continue going outward, without using part of the pleat allowance, and the skirt still looks like it's straight. (This also works at the straight side seams.) A pleat added to the offgrain seam hangs closed. Just keep in mind that if you make a straight skirt from striped fabric using this add-on technique, the stripes will form chevrons. This effect offers some interesting design possibilities, particularly if you decide to use an inverted pleat; if the underlay has chevrons pointing in the opposite direction from the pleat, the pleat/underlay combination forms a striking pattern.

The shape of your body has a lot to do with the amount that you need to add to take the seam offgrain. The smaller your waist is in relation to your hips, the more fabric you need to add; $3/8$ in. is the minimum I'd add to each seam allowance. If your waist is a size or two smaller than your hips, add more than $3/8$ in. and add to the straight side seams as well. Amounts from $3/8$ in. to about $3/4$ in. can be added and the skirt will still appear to be straight. These small additional amounts can make a dramatic difference even for bodies that usually don't look great in a straight skirt.

Always add a little more width than you think is necessary if you're working in the final fabric. Baste the skirt together, try it on, and look at the shape and length. You can always remove the extra.

Adding to the skirt width to take the seam offgrain also works for a long pleat in a coat or long jacket. If the coat or jacket is already flared, add $1\frac{1}{2}$ to 2 in. before the pleat allowance is added.

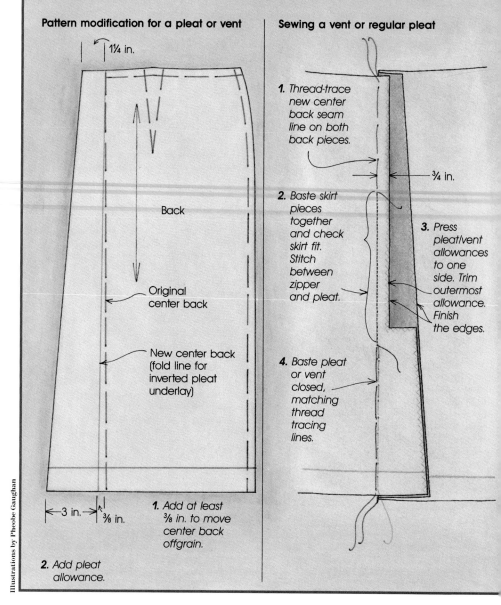

Pattern modification for a pleat or vent

1¼ in.

Back

Original center back

New center back (fold line for inverted pleat underlay)

3 in.

⅜ in.

1. Add at least ⅜ in. to move center back offgrain.

2. Add pleat allowance.

Illustrations by Phoebe Gaughan

Sewing a vent or regular pleat

1. Thread-trace new center back seam line on both back pieces.

¾ in.

2. Baste skirt pieces together and check skirt fit. Stitch between zipper and pleat.

3. Press pleat/vent allowances to one side. Trim outermost allowance. Finish the edges.

4. Baste pleat or vent closed, matching thread tracing lines.

Now for the pleat

Once you've set the seam offgrain, you'll add width to the skirt along its entire length to form the body of the pleat or vent. A pleat can be wider or narrower than 3 in. at the hem, but it should be at least 1¼ in. at the waist, which is just about right to hold the pleat up. If the addition at the waist is narrower than 1¼ in., you'll have to topstitch the pleat to hold it in place. Adding to the skirt width is the same for either a pleat or a vent.

You need to know exactly where the center back lines are throughout the construction process. After cutting the garment pieces from the fabric, I like to chalk the new center back on the wrong side of each piece, and then thread trace the chalk line. Chalking with a ruler makes a neat, straight line. The chalk will wear away but thread tracing shows on both sides of the fabric. Use a thread color that you won't be using for further basting or permanent stitching.

Pin the two skirt back pieces together,

matching the thread-traced lines. Baste the two pieces together, leaving the zipper and pleat opening unstitched. I baste by hand because the stitches are easier to remove than machine basting or any other machine stitching. I never machine stitch until I know I'm ready for permanent stitching. Besides, removing machine stitching can damage some fabrics.

Make sure that both sides of the zipper opening are the same length. Try the skirt on, decide on the height of the pleat/vent opening, then machine stitch the section of the seam between the zipper and the pleat/vent opening, as shown in the upper right drawing, and tie the thread ends. Don't stitch the horizontal line that marks the top of the pleat yet.

At this point, you'll treat the skirt differently depending on whether you're adding a regular pleat/vent or an inverted pleat. I'll cover the regular pleat/vent first. Press both pleat/vent allowances to one side (as you face the wrong side of the skirt, both

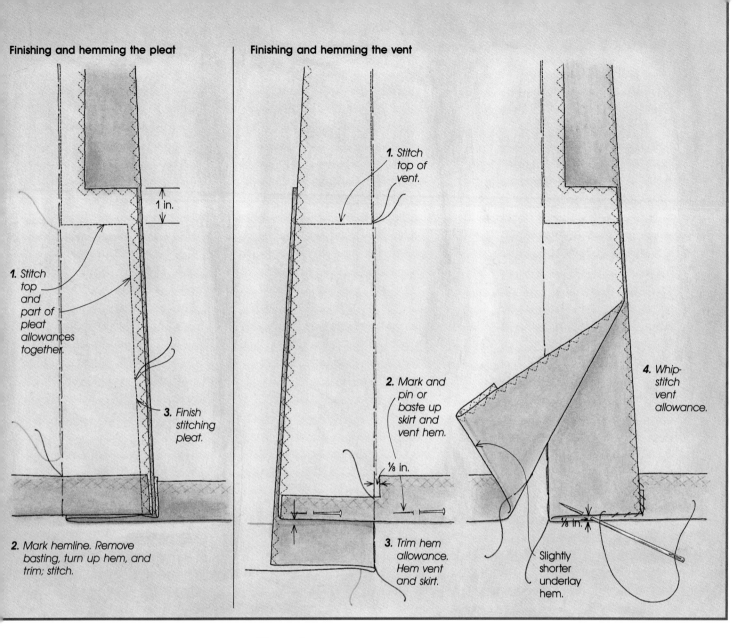

Finishing and hemming the pleat

1. Stitch top and part of pleat allowances together.

1 in.

3. Finish stitching pleat.

2. Mark hemline. Remove basting, turn up hem, and trim; stitch.

Finishing and hemming the vent

1. Stitch top of vent.

2. Mark and pin or baste up skirt and vent hem.

⅛ in.

3. Trim hem allowance. Hem vent and skirt.

4. Whip-stitch vent allowance.

⅛ in.

Slightly shorter underlay hem.

allowances are pressed to the right). Even if you have cut the fabric pieces precisely, the width of the allowances may not match, depending on how much fabric the turn of the cloth consumed. (This can also happen on the inverted pleat. When the underlay is placed over the pressed-open allowances, you might notice that they don't exactly match.) The important step is to make sure the allowances are lying flat.

Trim the uppermost layer of the pleat/vent allowance to ¾ in. until you reach a point 1 in. from the pleat/vent opening. Now use your favorite seam finish to make sure the edges don't ravel. I like to use a three-step zigzag, but a regular zigzag, machine or hand overcasting, or a binding would do as well.

Now machine stitch across the top of the vent and tie the thread ends. For the pleat, stitch across the top, pivot at the corner, and stitch down the sides to within 4 or 5 in. of where you think the hemline will be; tie off the threads.

Hemming

Although there are slight differences between the ways a pleat and a vent are hemmed, which are shown in the drawings above, the procedure for marking and trimming is the same. Before marking the hems, baste the vent or pleat closed so that the thread-traced center back lines meet. Try the skirt on and mark the hemline with chalk or basting; then remove the basting that closes the pleat/vent so you can turn up the hem allowance. Trim the allowance so that it's even all around, and pin or baste the hem up to check that the hemline is level.

Hem the skirt up to the pleat line. If you're putting in a pleat, hem it as well, as shown in the left drawing above. To finish the pleat, machine stitch the allowances together from the top to the hem.

While the body of a pleat is left to hang free, the folded flap of a vent is tacked down at the hem. To reduce the bulk, the vent's hem allowance is trimmed as shown in the center drawing above. Fold the vent

allowances to the left as seen from the inside of the skirt; you will see the hem allowance that will always be covered. Trim away half of the hem allowance from the finished edge to about ⅛ in. past the basted center back line. Fold the allowance back on itself and catchstitch the edge to the hem, being careful not to let the stitches go through to the front. Also raise the vent hem slightly so the underlay is shorter the overlay. The hem will look smooth on the outside of the skirt.

Inverted pleat

The patternmaking for an inverted pleat is the same as for the pleat/vent except that the pleat underlay requires a separate pattern piece. To make a pattern for the underlay, fold a piece of paper and place the fold on the new center back line of the skirt pattern. Trace the outline of the pleat shape, add 1 in. to the top for a seam allowance, mark the grainline, and cut the pattern out.

After cutting the fabric, mark and baste the center back lines of the skirt and the pleat underlay by chalking and thread tracing. Baste the skirt pieces together for a fitting, then machine stitch from the bottom of the zipper opening to the top of the pleat opening. Press the pleat allowances open.

Pin the underlay to the pleat with right sides together, and hand baste the underlay to the pleat around all sides, matching the center back thread tracings, as shown in the left drawing below. Machine stitch each side of the underlay to the pleat allowances from the center back to within 8 to 10 in. of the hemline.

Try on the skirt and mark the hem of the skirt and the underlay. Release part of the underlay basting so that you can turn up the hem, and trim the hem allowances so they are even all around. Stitch the skirt pleat and hem.

There's a neat trick to getting the hem of the pleat underlay to pull up slightly at the center hem, rather than hanging below the hem. Re-mark the hemline on the underlay ¼ in. higher than the previously marked hemline as shown in the top photo at left and the right drawing below. Cut ¼ in. from the hem allowance of the underlay. Release the basting that holds the underlay to the pleat allowances and hem the underlay. Stretch the underlay along its length until its new hemline and the skirt hemline match, as shown in the bottom photo below; then pin. Precise marking is important to the success of this trick—¼ in. isn't much and can easily get lost with careless or sloppy marking.

To finish the pleat, stitch the underlay to the pleat allowances. □

Linda Faiola is a patternmaker who teaches at the Cambridge Center for Adult Education in Cambridge, MA. Her previous articles on making a sloper and on pockets appeared in Threads, *issues No. 16 (pp. 56-61) and 13 (pp. 30-35) respectively.*

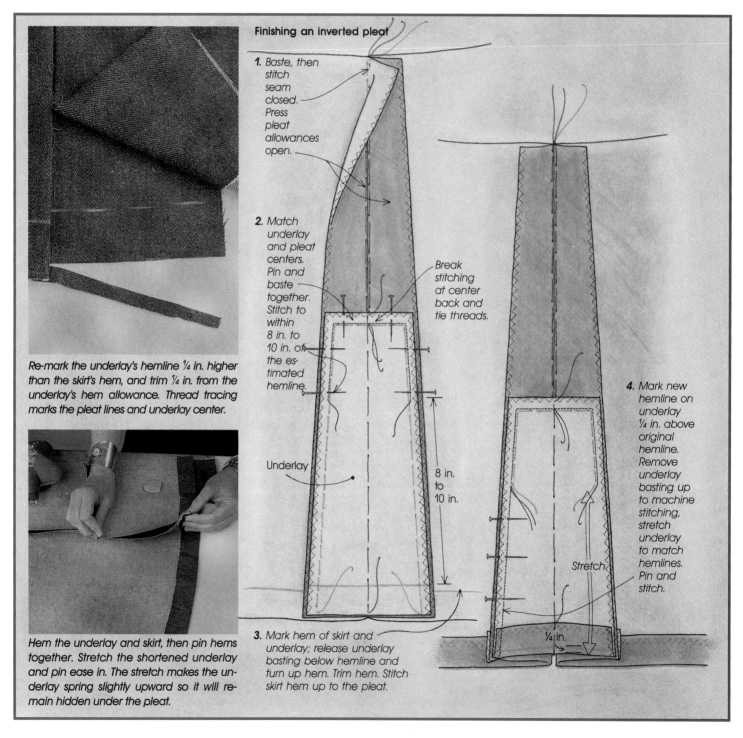

Re-mark the underlay's hemline ¼ in. higher than the skirt's hem, and trim ¼ in. from the underlay's hem allowance. Thread tracing marks the pleat lines and underlay center.

Hem the underlay and skirt, then pin hems together. Stretch the shortened underlay and pin ease in. The stretch makes the underlay spring slightly upward so it will remain hidden under the pleat.

Finishing an inverted pleat

1. Baste, then stitch seam closed. Press pleat allowances open.

2. Match underlay and pleat centers. Pin and baste together. Stitch to within 8 in. to 10 in. of the estimated hemline.

Break stitching at center back and tie threads.

Underlay

8 in. to 10 in.

3. Mark hem of skirt and underlay; release underlay basting below hemline and turn up hem. Trim hem. Stitch skirt hem up to the pleat.

4. Mark new hemline on underlay ¼ in. above original hemline. Remove underlay basting up to machine stitching, stretch underlay to match hemlines. Pin and stitch.

Stretch

¼ in.

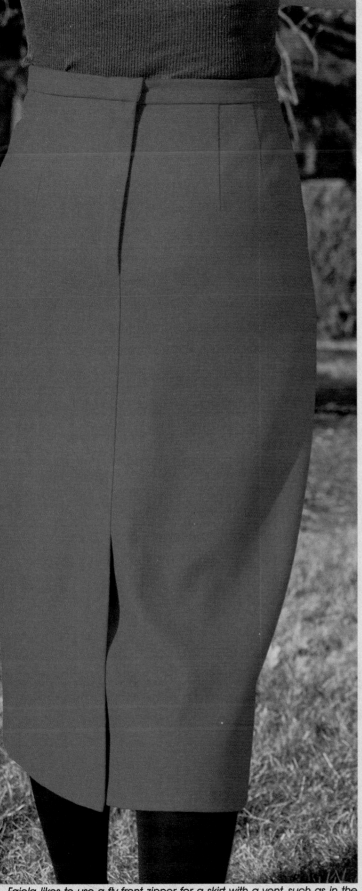

Faiola likes to use a fly-front zipper for a skirt with a vent, such as in the straight skirt above. The pleat allowances are folded to one side as shown in the photo of the opened zipper at right. The right zipper tape is stitched on top of the seam allowance.

A better zipper for a vent or pleat

My method of applying a lap zipper, which I call a fly zipper, is not traditional, but don't be afraid to try it. As you can see from the photo at lower right, half the zipper is stitched *on top* of the underlap seam allowance, rather than under the folded seam allowance. I developed this technique because I was looking for a way to keep both of the vent/pleat allowances folded flat to one side. Pattern instructions usually call for you to clip one seam allowance so you can press the allowances open, but clipping creates a point that could easily tear.

I am usually quite open to new ideas, but there is one aspect of zipper construction that I am inflexible about. I always work from the outside of the garment. My rule is, if the stitching shows on the outside, then do the work from the outside. I pin, baste, and permanently stitch while facing the outside of the skirt.

Close the zipper and place the tape edge ⅛ in. from the basted centerback line as shown in the drawing at right. Leave space at the zipper top for the waistband. Baste near the middle of the tape to hold the zipper to the seam allowance, and then machine stitch on the basting. (I always baste exactly where I will stitch.) Zigzag the edge of the zipper tape to the fabric; a three-step zigzag won't create a ridge of thread.

Now match the thread-traced center back lines of the skirt and pin them together; take up only ⅛ in. of fabric with each pin so that the lap remains flat. Accurately and precisely baste the other side of the zipper tape to the overlap through all layers, ⅞ in. from the center back; the basting should just clear the seam allowance of the underlap. Stitch the overlap by machine or hand from the outside of the skirt. Stitching across the bottom is optional. –L.F.

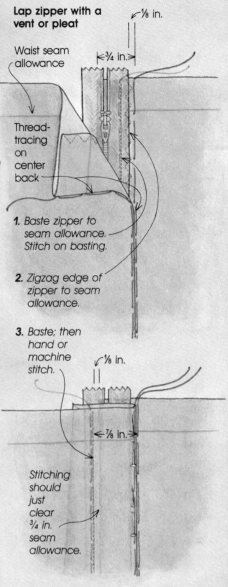

Lap zipper with a vent or pleat

Waist seam allowance

Thread-tracing on center back

⅛ in.

¾ in.

1. *Baste zipper to seam allowance. Stitch on basting.*

2. *Zigzag edge of zipper to seam allowance.*

3. *Baste; then hand or machine stitch.*

⅛ in.

⅞ in.

Stitching should just clear ¾ in. seam allowance.

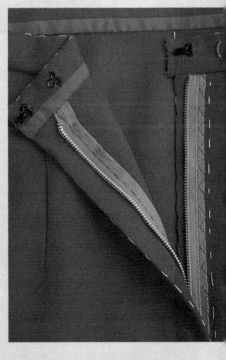

Buttoning Up
Draft a pattern alternative to the standard closure

by Linda Faiola

hen I was eight years old, my grandmother made me a sleeveless blue corduroy top with a skirt to match. I remember the outfit because it was unusual; the shirt buttoned along the side seam. No one else had anything like it, and it was my favorite.

A garment's closure is a place to be creative. At the same time, you want to make a garment that won't gap or pull, have buttons in the wrong place, or have buttons that will come undone. The trick is to choose the right closure for the job and make it work.

I'll discuss how to modify a pattern so that you can design your own closures with buttons and buttonholes. The fact is that not many closures, creative or otherwise, function as well as the versatile button-and-buttonhole. Start with the information in the following examples and expand and apply it to suit your own creative needs, as I did to make the jacket shown at left. You might consider creative closures on waistbands, hoods, shoulders, pockets, pegged jeans, cuffs, and even on knapsacks, backpacks, and pocketbooks.

Simplicity first

Most closures are simple enough and, if thought out and carefully planned, they don't need to be checked out in a test muslin garment, assuming you're confident that the pattern already fits. Refer to the drawings at right for a basic pattern modification and a look at the primary ingredients: style lines (where garments open), buttons, buttonholes, laps, and facings.

Plan placement of buttons, buttonholes, and the lap at the beginning of the pattern-work so the style lines meet exactly when the garment is buttoned. Ideally you'll have buttons on hand when making the pattern. ⇨

Jazz up garments by making buttons and closures part of the design, as Linda Faiola did for the front and sleeves of her rain jacket. (Photo by Yvonne Taylor)

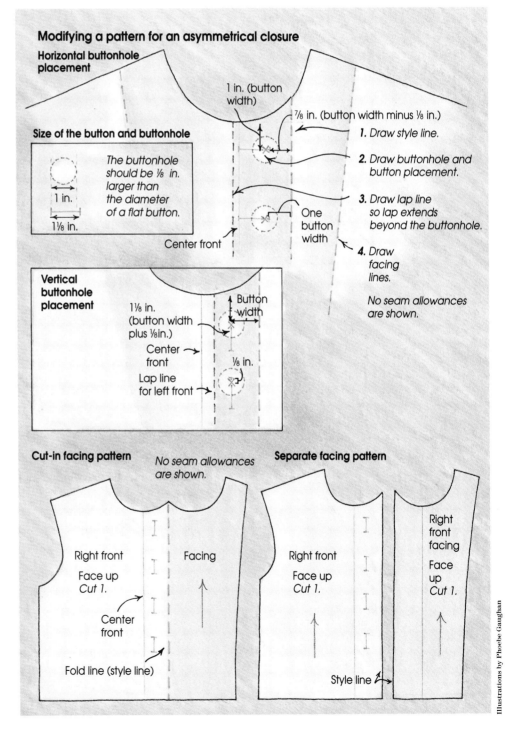

Modifying a pattern for an asymmetrical closure

Horizontal buttonhole placement

1 in. (button width)

⅞ in. (button width minus ⅛ in.)

1. Draw style line.
2. Draw buttonhole and button placement.
3. Draw lap line so lap extends beyond the buttonhole.
4. Draw facing lines.

No seam allowances are shown.

Center front

One button width

Size of the button and buttonhole

1 in.

1⅛ in.

The buttonhole should be ⅛ in. larger than the diameter of a flat button.

Vertical buttonhole placement

1⅛ in. (button width plus ⅛ in.)

Button width

Center front

⅛ in.

Lap line for left front

Cut-in facing pattern

No seam allowances are shown.

Right front
Face up
Cut 1.

Center front

Facing

Fold line (style line)

Separate facing pattern

Right front
Face up
Cut 1.

Right front facing
Face up
Cut 1.

Style line

Illustrations by Phoebe Gaughan

When the button size changes, the buttonhole changes, which in turn changes the lap width. I don't always have the buttons and you probably won't either. Don't despair; when you get to the information on laps, you'll see how to account for the unknown.

Style line—Deciding on what I call the *style line* is the first step in drafting the pattern for an asymmetrical closure. The style line is the design line that you draw on the pattern where the garment will eventually open. It can be straight, curved, scalloped, or any combination you can think of.

In the beginning stages of the patternwork, I superimpose the left and right fronts of the pattern, if it has a front closure, just as if the garment was buttoned. If the pattern is one piece, I draw on it as is.

In the excitement of design, don't forget the major construction problems you might be creating. Be aware of your limitations and your tolerances for working with picky sewing details and exotic fabrics. I have a category of details that I refer to as "Is the end product worth the aggravation?" If the answer to the question is "No," I reject the design.

Lap—The lap is just that, the extra fabric that laps under or over the two sides of the opening when the garment is fastened. Lap sizes are determined by the buttonhole placement and the size of the buttons. On symmetrical closures, the lap is added to both sides. For an asymmetrical closure on a woman's garment, the lap is added to the left front pattern to serve as an underlap.

The lap should extend entirely under the buttonhole and is most important to calculate correctly for horizontal buttonholes. When you know only the approximate size of the button, make the lap at least twice as wide as the button plus a little extra. You can make the lap extra generous, especially if you don't have the buttons yet.

Button placement—Buttons are sewn to the lap one button width in from the style line. They can be irregularly spaced or grouped with uneven spacing.

Place the buttons at stress points. The more fitted the garment, the more critical this is. A button at the bustline is less likely to allow gapping than a button above and below the bustline. Other stress points on a fitted garment are the waistline and hipline.

Size of the button is another consideration. Small buttons are usually easier to juggle and place than large buttons. They don't need to match but it helps if they are about the same size. Irregular buttons or ones with sharp edges can be difficult to work through the buttonhole. If you want to use unwieldy buttons, then position them where they don't need to be buttoned and

unbuttoned often. You'll have greater success if you don't put heavy buttons on lightweight fabrics.

Buttonholes—The buttonhole takes the stress, so plan the size carefully. If the button is flat and slippery, make the buttonhole about ⅛ in. longer than the button diameter. If the button is irregularly shaped, thick, domed, or not slippery (cloth covered, for example), then make a test buttonhole to determine the correct length. This is also a good time to check that you can make a presentable buttonhole in the fabric, before you decide that buttonholes and buttons are the way to go.

Buttonholes can be perpendicular or parallel to an edge, or placed at an angle; there are no rules. But consider the function. A shirt band, with its strong vertical lines, should have buttonholes parallel to the band. On the shoulder closure shown in the drawing on page 28, perpendicular buttonholes will keep the garment closed better than if they were parallel to the opening. If you try an angled buttonhole, make sure you work your sample on the same grain.

Buttons slide to the end of the buttonholes and the shanks take up space. That's why a horizontal buttonhole begins ⅛ in. closer to the style line than the button placement, and vertical buttonholes start about ⅛ in. higher. For horizontal buttonholes, the first is placed at least one button width down from the finished neck edge.

Patterns—I label asymmetrical patterns "face up" to avoid making cutting mistakes. Face up means to lay the fabric and pattern out with right sides up. A face-up marking assures that you will cut a correct right front and left front, and that the garment will close on the side you want.

Be sure to indicate the grainline on any pattern you make. The grainline determines how the garment will hang, so every pattern should have one. (For more on tracing patterns, see *Threads*, No. 33, p. 20). On patterns for asymmetrical closures, draw a grainline with one arrow, instead of arrows at both ends. This indicates that all pieces must be laid out in the same direction on the fabric, which is very important for directional fabrics such as corduroy, velvet, or a print with trees all growing in the same direction.

Facings can be cut as one with the body or created as separate patterns (bottom drawing, p. 25). Cut-in facings work best when the fabric is bulky, loosely woven, or unstable, but they can be used only when the style line is straight. Cut-in facings will make the pattern pieces larger, which may require extra fabric. When you are drawing lines for the facing outline, avoid overlapping a facing edge with a lap edge. The edge

A shaped edge

The pattern shown in the drawing on the facing page works—although one could argue that the design is less than great—but it's interesting in terms of a patternmaking lesson. I wanted something asymmetrical but more interesting than an off-center, straight front closure.

As I drew sketches, I thought about scallops: whether they should be the same size and how many there would be. I drew a straight line as a guide for the wavy style line where I wanted the closure to be, then roughly sketched the scallops in a size arrangement that I liked. A French curve helped to outline the scallops smoothly and to draw the flattened S-curve along the neckline. The scallops are, at their widest point, at least as wide as one button width, measured from the original dotted line.

The button placements came next. Since the garment is not fitted, I could place the buttons casually. If the garment was fitted, I would use more and smaller scallops so that the buttons could be strategically placed.

I included the button nearest to the neckline so that the closing would be smooth and decided on one that would blend into the fabric. The scallop buttons would be different sizes and types that would look good together.

The buttonholes just seemed to fall into place; they looked best if they were perpendicular to the style line. After I marked the positions of the buttons and buttonholes, I could see how far the lap for the left front had to extend. The lap stops short of the right shoulder for less bulk.

The facing lines came next and forced me to think about the hemline. I chose facings that would work for a top to be sewn to a band or skirt; the hemline could be gathered or straight. If I had wanted a jacket or a top, I would have had to add a facing to the hemline, or I would have extended the bottom with a hem allowance. The edges of the left-front underlap and the right-front facing do not coincide.

The final patterns for the fronts and facings are shown in the lower drawings. The jacket on p. 24 has a closure that is drafted in the same way as the scallops. –L.F.

Asymmetrical scallop closure

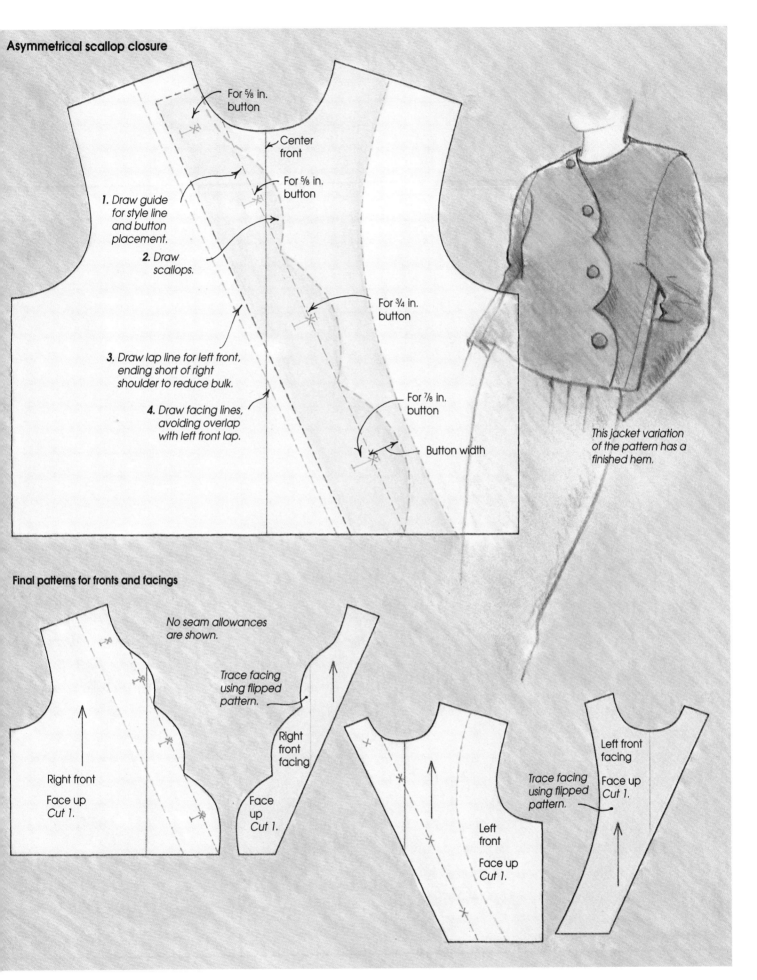

For ⅝ in. button

Center front

For ⅝ in. button

1. Draw guide for style line and button placement.

2. Draw scallops.

For ¾ in. button

3. Draw lap line for left front, ending short of right shoulder to reduce bulk.

4. Draw facing lines, avoiding overlap with left front lap.

For ⅞ in. button

Button width

This jacket variation of the pattern has a finished hem.

Final patterns for fronts and facings

No seam allowances are shown.

Trace facing using flipped pattern.

Right front

Face up
Cut 1.

Right front facing

Face up
Cut 1.

Left front

Face up
Cut 1.

Trace facing using flipped pattern.

Left front facing

Face up
Cut 1.

of the right facing, for example, should not be right on top of the left underlap edge.

Facings work better if the grain matches the body's. If the style line is not parallel to the grain, a cut-in facing may not work. Separate facings can be cut from another fabric, which could be less bulky, or of another color.

Pay close attention to the way the facings are labeled. Separate facings have to be mirror images of the body pattern if the fabric's right side is different from its wrong side.

On the shoulder

A shoulder opening (pattern draft sequence is shown below) is one solution for a garment with a neckline that's too small to go over the head and that doesn't have an opening at the center front or back. I am right-handed, so I prefer a left shoulder closure, with a style line forward of the shoulder seam. If you keep the style line within 1½ in. of the shoulder seam, you

can remove the seam on that side. This draft works best for patterns without shoulder darts, so that the shoulder seamlines are straight.

Draw the style line parallel to the shoulder on the front pattern. Cut on the line and add the piece to the back, lapping the shoulder lines if the pattern has seam allowances. Follow the guidelines for perpendicular buttonholes (top drawing, p. 25) and draft the asymmetrical pattern and facings. The finished front and back patterns (right-hand drawings, below) have facings cut with the body; front and back neck facings complete the patterns.

Removable buttons

The closure shown in the photo and pattern draft on the facing page allows you to remove the buttons easily, which creates some interesting advantages. Some buttons cannot survive the cleaners or the washer and

dryer. And, like me, you might have a vast collection of buttons. With this design, a simple shirt can have a variety of looks.

Each shirt front has a set of buttonholes. This might be my imagination, but if one set is horizontal and the other is vertical, they seem to hold the buttons in place better than if both sets were vertical. Both sides could have horizontal buttonholes, but they have to be placed with precision.

The buttonholes are spaced 2½ in. apart while the buttons are spaced 2⅝ in. apart. The spacing allows for some play so that there is no buckling. The width of the ribbon is optional, but I'd choose one approximately the button width. Grosgrain widths are limited, so you have to be flexible. □

Linda Faiola's article on pleats for straight skirts appeared in Threads *No. 30. She is a patternmaker who teaches at the Cambridge Center for Adult Education in Cambridge, MA.*

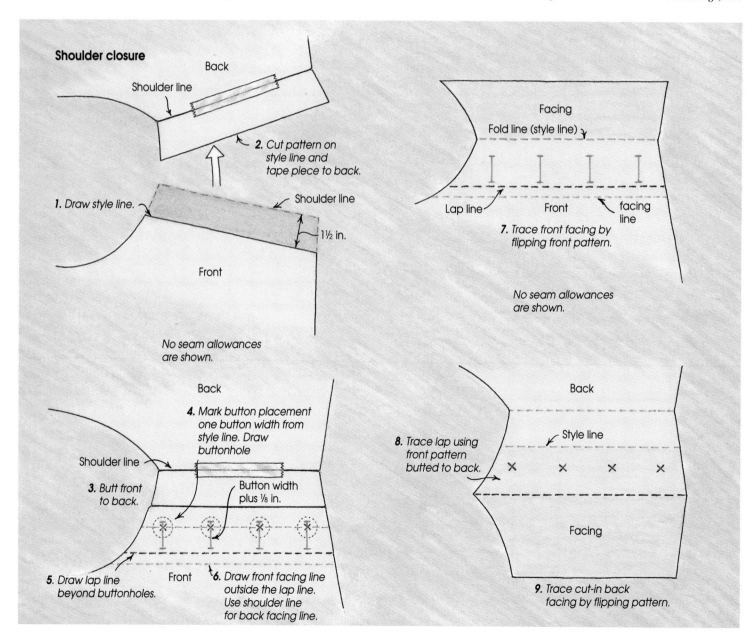

Shoulder closure

Back
Shoulder line
2. Cut pattern on style line and tape piece to back.

1. Draw style line.
Shoulder line
1½ in.
Front
No seam allowances are shown.

Facing
Fold line (style line)
Lap line — Front — facing line
7. Trace front facing by flipping front pattern.

No seam allowances are shown.

Back
4. Mark button placement one button width from style line. Draw buttonhole
Shoulder line
3. Butt front to back.
Button width plus ⅛ in.
5. Draw lap line beyond buttonholes.
Front
6. Draw front facing line outside the lap line. Use shoulder line for back facing line.

Back
Style line
8. Trace lap using front pattern butted to back.
Facing
9. Trace cut-in back facing by flipping pattern.

Black goes with any color, so why limit the button options? Both the left and right fronts of this unisex shirt have buttonholes. To switch buttons, Faiola selects a set already sewn to a grosgrain ribbon. The birds are taken from a '60's bracelet.

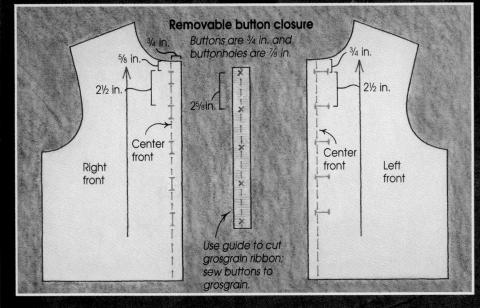

Removable button closure

Buttons are ¾ in. and buttonholes are ⅞ in.

¾ in.
⅝ in.
2½ in.

Right front

Center front

2⅝ in.

×
×
×
×
×
×

Use guide to cut grosgrain ribbon; sew buttons to grosgrain.

¾ in.
2½ in.

Center front

Left front

Making a Kilt

Sew a man's traditional kilt or a woman's kilt skirt

by Ann Stewart

When I was 15, I apprenticed as a tailor in Elgin, Scotland. I think I wanted to sew like my grandmother ever since I was born. Before I was allowed to sew my first buttonhole on a man's fly, I did 130 practice buttonholes in scrap fabric. I've been handmaking kilts for more than 30 years.

The kilt is a very warm garment, and because Scotland is so cold, with wet, fierce winds nearly all winter, all the girls wore kilts or kilt skirts when I was growing up. The boys only wore them for special occasions. Today men's kilts are more popular in the United States than they are in Scotland; the average Scotsman doesn't think of a kilt until he wants to get married.

The man's traditional kilt, made from an eight-yard length of fabric, is deeply pleated in the back; the unpleated front overlaps from hip to hip, and the outside front edge is fringed. The kilt closes with a buckle on each side of the waist below the narrow waistband. Some women, myself included, prefer the traditional kilt's fullness to the woman's kilt skirt, which is made with half as much fabric. A lady's kilt skirt closes on the left, a traditional kilt on the right—even if a woman intends to wear it. The other differences between the man's kilt and woman's kilt skirt arise from handling the greatly different quantities of fabric and from tailoring to a male or female shape. In this article, I'll explain how to construct a traditional kilt, but I'll also describe the kilt skirt.

Tartan fabrics

Much research goes into finding the correct clan or district tartan. There are hundreds of different tartans, and the same tartan from different mills will look different because the tones of the standard colors will vary. Some of the large clan tartans like Stewart have well over a dozen variations. And many tartans have "hunting" and "dress" versions. The mills I deal with produce tartans in modern, bright colors as well as in muted "ancient" colors. Kilts made of identical tartan can also look very different because of the way they're pleated. The tartan is pleated to the stripe (usually a narrow, strong vertical line in the pattern) for regimental kilts, which are worn by Scottish regiments and by bagpipe bands. For dress kilts, the tartan is reproduced in the pleats so you see the pattern as if the fabric had not been pleated.

The mills in Scotland weave a wide variety of tartans in a double-width fabric (54 to 60 in.), which is symmetrical at the fold. If they don't have a tartan in stock, the mills I deal with will custom-weave the desired length of special tartan in single-width (27 in.) fabric, usually within six weeks.

Most tartans are woven with fine, smooth, worsted wool in a simple 2-by-2 twill fabric. Tartan weights suitable for kilts range anywhere from 11 oz. to 19 oz., with the middle range providing the best compromise between hang and bulk. I like to use 13-oz. tartan for a man's kilt and 11-oz. for a woman's. Nine-ounce tartan is really too light, but when I must make a kilt with it, I get an extra yard and put in extra pleats. It's fine for childrenswear. "Saxony" wool tartans are too soft and clingy to hang and wear well as kilts. I can also get any tartan woven 30 in. wide in 100% silk for ladies' eveningwear.

The repeat pattern of a tartan is called the sett, shown in the photos at right. You designate a sett as the distance from the center of one square to the center of the next identical square or as the distance from one line to the same line on the next square in a full pattern repeat.

Since each tartan is different, very few have the same sett width. Most setts are symmetrical; but a few, like the Buchanan (top photo at right), have a "one-way" sett, and you have to be particularly careful in working with them. Lamont is another interesting type of sett, a "double sett;" if you look closely at the example at bottom right, you'll notice that the full sett repeat is twice as wide as it at first appears.

Since most kilts are assembled from double-width tartan, the tartan is cut in half lengthwise, leaving several inches along the length of the fold for waistband, tabs, and sash. The halves are joined at a center back seam. It's very important to mark the wrong side of both pieces with tailor's chalk before cutting and sewing. On the right side of the fabric, the twill rib goes upward toward the left.

Planning a kilt

For a traditional kilt you'll need eight yards of single-width or four yards of double-width tartan. See "Sources," p. 34.

After pleating the back half of the kilt, hand sewing the pleats, and self-facing the front edges, you interface the pleats of a man's kilt before attaching the rolled waistband and closures. A traditional kilt is also lined. The hem is the selvage. So in addition to the tartan, you'll need a piece of hair canvas or linen 1½ times your hip width and 8 in. to 10 in. wide, a yard of fine cotton lining material, and a pair of straps and buckles.

The first step is to take accurate measurements of your waist, widest part of your hip, length from waist to hip, and overall length. For a traditional man's kilt,

measure not from the waist but from the top of the haunch bone, adding a 2-in. rise to reach the waistband seam allowance. When a man kneels on the floor, his kilt should be one inch off the floor.

With the wrong side marked, cut your tartan to length and straight along the grain, as shown at lower left in the drawing on p. 32. You'll need a 5-in. to 6-in. width of the extra fabric at the fold for the waistband and buckle tabs.

Lay a piece of tartan on the table, right side up, with selvage to the right. Start at the farthest raw edge, which will be the under-apron. The kilt will close on the right. Choose a predominant line in your tartan to be the center front on both aprons. Predominant lines in tartan are usually the narrow single or double bright-colored stripes. Allow an extra three to five inches on the edge for facing. Mark one-quarter of your hip measurement on each side of the center front line at the hipline, as shown in the top drawing, pp. 32-33. Also mark one-quarter of your waist measurement on each side of the center front at the waistline. At the selvage (hemline), make a mark on each side of the center front one inch wider than the hip marks. This allows a slight A-line flare to improve the hang. Allow a slightly narrower flare if the kilt is for a man. Join the marks from waist to hip to hemline (lower left drawing, p. 33).

The over-apron, at the other end of the

Non-symmetrical one-way setts like Buchanan, above, are rare. Lamont (below) is a double-sett tartan. This one repeats only every 12¼ inches, which would result in very few, very deep pleats, so Stewart pleats half setts.

With its seven yards of pleats, a man's kilt is the ultimate pleated skirt—in Royal Stewart or any tartan imaginable. (Photo by Yvonne Taylor)

Kilt layout

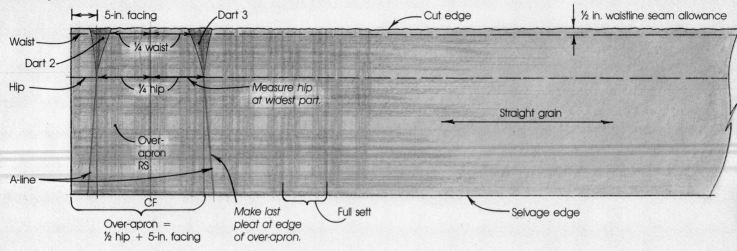

- 5-in. facing
- Dart 3
- Cut edge
- ½ in. waistline seam allowance
- Waist
- Dart 2
- ¼ waist
- Hip
- ¼ hip
- Measure hip at widest part.
- Over-apron RS
- Straight grain
- A-line
- CF
- Over-apron = ½ hip + 5-in. facing
- Make last pleat at edge of over-apron.
- Full sett
- Selvage edge

Preparing the tartan

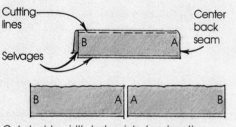

- Cutting lines
- Center back seam
- Selvages
- B
- A
- B   A   A   B

Cut double-width tartan into two lengths, but don't sew center back seam yet.

For test-pleating, Stewart makes chalk marks about ⅝ in. apart across one full sett.

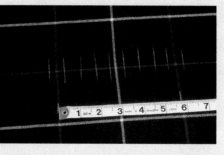

Pleating cross section

- Dart 4
- CB
- Facing
- Fringe
- First regular pleat, double sett
- Dart 1
- Under-apron
- Dart 3
- Dart 2
- Inverted pleat, double sett
- CF
- Over-apron
- Last pleat, double sett

There are three ways to pleat a kilt. Dress kilts are pleated to reproduce the pattern sett, as the swatch of Royal Stewart at left illustrates. For a regimental tartan and kilt (center), you pleat so that the narrow, bright strip is centered on every pleat, as in this Lamont. Or you can pleat to the square, choosing one portion of the sett and centering it on every pleat, as Stewart has done for her Black Stewart kilt skirt (right). This method is only used on kilt skirts where the pleats are fewer in number and wider. Traditional kilts always display either dress or regimental pleating.

Hand-felted Jackets for Kids

Seamless garments from a few wool fibers and a little soapy water

by Anne Einset Vickrey

Anne Vickrey's son is obviously delighted with his handmade, seamless felted jacket; instructions, from fitting the pattern to dyeing the garment, start at right. (Photo by author)

even though I'd been making small felt wearables for several years, I was still hesitant to make a felt jacket because I thought it would take too much time and muscle. Smaller always means easier in feltmaking, so I finally decided I might be able to manage a jacket for my two-year-old son. Once I'd developed a pattern that worked, I was surprised at how easy it is to make a seamless garment like the one my son is wearing on p. 37. After arranging the wool, it takes me only three to four hours to form the fabric into a child's jacket.

About felting

Felt is formed when wool fibers become bonded through exposure to heat, moisture, and pressure or agitation. With enough pressure, agitation isn't necessary; the scales along each wool fiber cause the fibers to interlock when they're pressed together. Hot water softens the fibers, and a little soap helps them to slide easily over each other; once interlocked, it's almost impossible to unlock them. If you put a layer of plastic between two layers of carded wool, you can exert pressure to felt the wool on either side and the plastic will keep the layers from fusing. To form a jacket, I simply sandwich a flat, jacket-shaped piece of plastic between layers of wool. The jacket has no visible seams because I overlap and felt the wool at the edges where the front and back layers meet just outside the plastic pattern.

Knit or woven fabric felts when agitated, and it always shrinks at the same time, because the hot, wet fibers relax and compress in all directions and interlock in their relaxed position. But when you make felt by pressing on carded wool, the shrinkage is not in length and width, only in depth. You're compressing the loose fibers into a thinner and tougher fabric without greatly affecting the fabric's shape, and that's how you can make a jacket close to the size of the original pattern. The completed jacket is lightweight, warm, soft, durable, and not at all stiff.

Choosing and preparing wool

The type of wool you use is very important for successful feltmaking, especially if you're felting by hand. You need wool that felts quickly, and the best way to find that out is by testing. Before starting a jacket, test the wool by making a small, flat piece of felt according to the basic instructions that I give below. The wool should begin to felt in two to three minutes, but certainly no more than five minutes. For my jackets I use a blend of domestic wools from various sheep breeds, including Lincoln crossbreeds and Dorset. However, many breeds may be used for felting. I've gotten some good results with a blend of a lustrous, fairly coarse wool and a medium to fine wool.

You can do the carding by hand, but I prefer to use commercially-carded wool when I'm making a jacket because that's the easiest way to achieve a uniform felt. For companies that sell usable batts, see Sources on p. 41. Carding companies send washed wool through huge carding machines that arrange the fibers into comforter-size batts. The advantages are that the fibers end up lying in the same direction, and extremely thin layers of wool can be peeled off the batt in the sizes you need to fit the pattern.

Adjusting the jacket pattern

The basic jacket pattern I use is shown below. You can adjust it for size by varying the chest width; measure around your child's chest in inches, directly under the arms. Divide that number by two, then add 4 in. This is the width of your pattern under the arms. Add or subtract from my pattern to get the width you need by spreading or overlapping it at center front. Adjust the length and width of the sleeves and the length of the jacket for your child. I measure the arm from center back at the neckline to the wrist with the arm out straight, allowing an extra inch (more if I plan a turn-back cuff). I measure the length along the center back from neck to crotch.

To make your final pattern, first cut the adjusted shape out of a large piece of paper. Then tape the paper pattern to a piece of heavy plastic, such as a garbage can liner, and cut out the pattern in plastic. In addition, cut out a piece of plastic that covers just the body of the jacket; it will lie between the two front sections of the jacket so that you can create an overlapping front.

Making jacket batts

After you've cut your pattern, calculate the amount of wool you'll need for the jacket by folding the paper pattern in half along the center back and estimating with a ruler the surface area in square inches of the half-pattern. Multiply the number you get by two to get the total surface area of the jacket pattern. Divide the total number of square inches by 30 and that will give you the number of ounces of wool needed for the jacket.

The next step is to arrange the carded wool into jacket-shaped batts—one for the back and two for the fronts. Use 40% of the total amount of wool for the back, and 30% for each front. Each batt should have eight to ten layers of wool, with the fibers in each layer lying perpendicular to the fibers in the next layer. Peel off thin layers from your quilt batt and lay them over the plastic pattern. The wool should extend 3 to 4 in. out from the edge of the pattern, as shown in the drawing on p. 39 and taper slightly at the edges; these are the areas where the front and back batts will be joined together. Tear—don't cut—the layers to even the edges. Shape the fronts the same as the back; just leave off one sleeve each time, and make the opening edge vertical, as in the lower drawing on p. 39.

As you make the batts, use three or four more layers of wool on the body of the jacket than on the sleeves by interspersing body-only layers between layers that cover

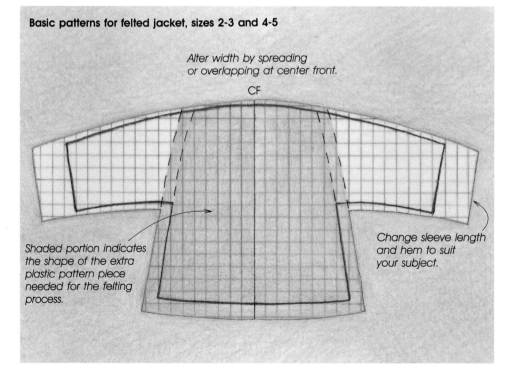

Basic patterns for felted jacket, sizes 2-3 and 4-5

Alter width by spreading or overlapping at center front.

CF

Shaded portion indicates the shape of the extra plastic pattern piece needed for the felting process.

Change sleeve length and hem to suit your subject.

the whole pattern. This helps insure against thin spots or holes on the jacket body and makes the sleeves more flexible.

Enveloping the pattern in wool

With three batts made, you're ready to begin shaping them around the pattern. For this process, you'll need a large surface area that can get wet; I use a Ping-Pong table covered with a tarp, but it needn't be that big. Have plenty of hot water available to mix with soap. I find I use 6 to 8 qt. of hot, soapy water just to wet down the batts for a size 4 child's jacket. To prepare the water, add ¼ cup of soap powder or flakes to 2 qt. of water that is as hot as your hands can stand when you're wearing rubber gloves. I mix the water in 4-qt. batches.

Wetting the back – Begin by laying down the back batt and centering your plastic pattern over it. Set the other two batts aside so they don't get wet. With the water nearby, scoop up cupfuls and carefully wet down the wool under the entire pattern so that it lies flat. Add just enough to dampen the wool but not so much that it runs beyond the area you're working on. It's important not to wet the wool that extends out from the edge of the pattern because these fibers will form the joins between front and back, and layers of wet fibers don't felt easily to other wet layers. I lift the pattern and pour a couple of cups of water in the center of the area the pattern covers. Then I put the pattern back and wet the plastic down on top so it's slippery. Thus, I can spread the water underneath out to the pattern edges by pressing on the pattern. Next, I fold the wool at the sleeve openings and waist under the pattern and wet it down so the pattern lies flat in those areas.

Attaching the fronts – Working only on one-half of the back pattern, fold the dry wool edge over onto the pattern and dampen it with hot, soapy water so that it stays folded. As shown in the top photo on p. 40, work up one side, around the sleeve, and over toward the center back, filling in the underarm with scrap wool. At the center back, leave the edge wool unfolded; this area will become the collar and neckline, and to keep it from becoming distorted, it's a good idea to leave it undefined until you attach the fronts.

Align one of the two smaller batts over the side of the pattern you have just been working on. At the sleeve opening and at the waist, wet down the wool inside the edge of the pattern. At the waist hem, fold the dry wool edge back onto itself. At the sleeve, fold the dry wool under the dampened front batt. Then, while dampening the wool directly over the pattern, wet down the first front batt with hot, soapy water and fold the remaining dry wool un-

der onto the back of the jacket, as in the lower photo on p. 40.

Along the top of the jacket, fold the dry wool under all the way to the center neck. Dampen the wool about 1 in. in from the edge of the front opening to form the collar and front of the jacket, as shown, or shape it in some other way you prefer. Fold the dry wool under to achieve an even edge.

Place the second piece of plastic from your pattern over the body of the jacket to protect the layers you've been working on. Then repeat the steps to attach the other front side of the jacket. Now you're ready to turn the matted wool fibers into felt.

Felting

If you try to lift any part of the jacket now, it will stretch out and fall apart because nothing is holding the fibers together. It is important at this point to work gently in order to keep the shape of the jacket intact. Exerting too much pressure on the fibers too early, when they aren't yet bonded, will spread the wool and result in a jacket that's too large. But if you don't increase the pressure after the felting has started, it'll take you forever to achieve a wearable felted material.

Begin felting by simply pushing directly down on the top layer of the jacket with your hands flat. Don't push on the edges or seams, because the jacket will stretch and you'll lose control of the shape. The wool should be saturated with hot, soapy water so that the fibers won't stick to your hands. I keep a sponge handy to pick up excess water that's seeping beyond the jacket.

Start with gentle pressure, and gradually increase the pressure until you notice a change in the fibers and feel that the top front layer is beginning to hold together. At this point, place one hand under just the top layer, and with your other hand on top, squeeze the wet wool. Do this over the first side of the front of the jacket, then fold it gently back and repeat the whole process on the other front.

Work the arms in the same way. After the entire front of the jacket is holding together, work on the seams. With one hand inside, gently press the seam areas between your hands, moving your top hand slightly while exerting pressure on the fibers between your hands. Fold back the two front sides of the jacket and begin to work on the back by pressing down on top of the pattern with your hands flat. Work in this manner for several minutes to start felting the fibers beneath the pattern.

To felt the back, you have to turn the jacket over, but because it's still saturated with water, it's too heavy to move without pulling apart. To get rid of the water, lay a large cloth (half of an old sheet is perfect) over the jacket and roll it up so that the

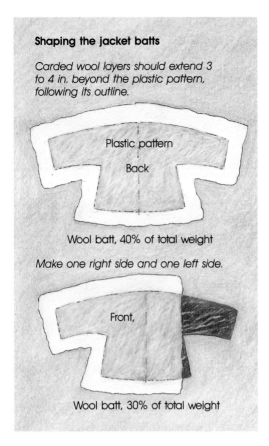

Shaping the jacket batts

Carded wool layers should extend 3 to 4 in. beyond the plastic pattern, following its outline.

Plastic pattern

Back

Wool batt, 40% of total weight

Make one right side and one left side.

Front,

Wool batt, 30% of total weight

cloth separates the layers as you roll it; then put the roll in the washing machine and spin it. When you carefully unroll the jacket after spinning, lay it down with the back up. Add more hot, soapy water and work on the back just as you did the front.

When the whole back starts to feel felted, work on the shoulders and other areas that were difficult to reach without lifting the jacket. You can remove the plastic pattern pieces now, but work carefully. The felt is pretty strong, but the jacket can still be stretched if you treat it too roughly. You need to toughen and slightly shrink it before it will be wearable. This is achieved in the fulling process, which we'll do next, but sometimes it's a good idea to turn the whole thing inside out–permanently–before fulling. The inner surface is often smoother, and it's definitely smaller than the outside.

Fulling

For hand felt-makers, fulling refers to the process of shrinking and further compacting felt by rubbing it on a washboard or something similar, like the corrugated drain area of a sink. This is what makes the felt durable enough to wear. During the fulling process, the felt will shrink and toughen rapidly until it becomes a firm, strong material. As before, the firmer it gets, the more pressure you need to apply to get the desired results, but you should start gently.

Work with the arms of the jacket perpendicular to the ribs of the washboard as I'm doing in the right-hand photo on p. 40. This way, the slight shrinkage won't shorten the

After wetting the garment back under the plastic pattern, Vickrey wets and folds the seam wool for half the garment onto the pattern, above. Below, Vickrey has shaped the batt for one side of the garment and folded the seam overlap to the back.

Vickrey arranged the felted jacket lengthwise on a washboard to begin the fulling process; fulling makes the felt durable enough to wear by further compacting the wool fibers.

Surface Design on Handmade Felt

by Karen Livingstone and Anne Einset Vickrey

Handmade felt can be colored with dyes or textile paints. Here are some techniques we've used with these two coloring agents.

Using textile paints

We suggest that you practice any technique you plan to use on a sample piece of felt in order to find out how much paint you need to get the look you want. Block, dry, and dye the felt first; then iron it to flatten the surface fibers before you apply paint.

Printing clear images on felt requires lots of paint, applied firmly with a hard object. You can also get lovely soft effects by using less paint and applying it with paper or sponges. Block printing can be done with Plexiglas, wood, or linoleum blocks, and even with carved potatoes. We used children's discarded plastic blocks in various shapes to block print on a child's jacket and made mittens and a beret to match (see photo on p. 41). We dipped the blocks into a dish of pigment straight from the jar and pressed the block against the felt for about five seconds.

When you've completed your design, follow the paint instructions for setting the pigment. This usually involves allowing the paint to dry for 24 hours and then ironing over it to set it into the fabric. It's easy to scorch the felt, so always use a press cloth. When the pigment has been set, hand wash or dry clean the garment.

Dyeing felt

We used weak acid dyes, like Deka Series L or Telana (see Sources on p. 41) to dye the jackets because they're easy to find and use, and they can dye wool relatively quickly. You'll need a dyepot that is large enough to hold the jacket comfortably without crowding, which can cause irregular dye coverage. Be sure to wear a dust mask and rubber gloves.

If you're dyeing the jacket a solid color, wet it first in warm water for about ten minutes, and then spin out the extra water in a washing machine before placing the jacket

jacket; instead, it'll bring in the sides for a better fit. Always work on a single layer of felt on the washboard. Add hot, soapy water, and with both hands flat on top of the felt, gently push down in one area, moving the fabric back and forth over the washboard about ¼ in. each way. It's almost more like vibrating the jacket than rubbing it. Gradually increase the pressure as you work on one spot for about 30 seconds. Then move the material so you can work on another area. Be sure to add more fresh, hot, soapy water as you go so that the felt moves easily over the washboard. Work evenly this way over the total area of the jacket. When you're finished, you should notice that the fabric is a little tougher. Repeat the procedure again; however, this time exert more pressure and rub the material a little more.

At this stage the felt will be strong enough so that you can rinse the jacket in a large basin of water and spin it dry. With most of the soap and water removed, you'll be able to see areas that need further work. Areas that may have stretched out, like the bottom of the jacket and the sleeve opening, can be shrunk by adding more hot, soapy water and rubbing the area over a larger part of the washboard in the direction that you want the material to shrink.

During this final shaping, continue to rinse the jacket and check where more fulling is required. When you're finished, rinse the jacket thoroughly in cool water, spin it dry, and blot it between towels. Try it on the child you made it for and decide

where buttons or closures will be. Then trim any uneven edges and work the cut edges with hot, soapy water to felt them uniformly. Rinse out the soap again, and let the jacket dry. The last steps are blocking and finishing, but if you want to change the jacket's color, now's the time to do so. You'll find some dyeing ideas at right, in "Surface Design on Handmade Felt."

Blocking and washing

Whether you have dyed your jacket or left it natural, you should block it before you bind the edges (an optional finishing touch) or add closures. To do this, set your iron on a wool setting and press the felt with a wet press cloth. Work over the entire surface of the jacket, dampening the cloth often. This smoothes and softens the material. At this point, the collar and lapels should be pressed; they will stay in the blocked position when allowed to dry.

You can clean the jacket like any other wool garment. Dry cleaning works well, and so does hand washing in cool water using a mild soap or detergent. If you wash it, avoid agitating the jacket too much, so that it doesn't shrink. After rinsing it, spin it in a washing machine to remove most of the water and blot it between towels. Shape the jacket and allow it to dry flat, and then re-block it as before. □

Anne Einset Vickrey is the author of Felting By Hand *(1987), available for $14 from Craft Works Publishing, Box 211, Menlo Park, CA 94026.*

Plastic blocks that are dipped in textile paints are ideal printing tools for making clear images on spongy felt.

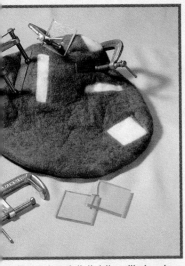

Clamping felt tightly with heat-resistant Plexiglas keeps the dye from coloring the clamped areas. The jacket below was dyed yellow, clamped, and overdyed blue.

in the dyebath. As you heat the dyebath, poke the felt around in the bath occasionally, but avoid vigorous stirring to prevent further felting or shrinking. Leave the wool in the dyebath and continue to check it occasionally for color intensity; this may take up to an hour or more. Then remove the jacket from the dyepot and rinse it out in warm water.

Dip dyeing is the technique of folding and dipping different parts of the jacket into the dyebath so that they are dyed different colors. We folded a jacket so that all the edges were aligned (see the drawing below); that way, we were able to hold the edges in one color dyebath and then dip the body in another color. We had to mix a strong dye solution (about 1 oz. of dye per lb. of wool) and acetic acid (vinegar, as described in the dye instructions) with the dye before dipping in order to get a reasonable color in about five minutes.

Folding and clamping sections of the felted jacket is an effective technique. We used shapes made from heat-resistant Plexiglas and clamped them onto the felt using small C-clamps; the clamped shapes act as a barrier to the dye. Shapes of wood also work well. Be sure the clamps are clean and rust-free so they don't stain the felt.

Put the shaped Plexiglas piece over the felt, and line it up with another piece of Plexiglas of the same shape under the material, as in the middle photo at left. Or, fold the felt and sandwich two layers between three shapes. You may need to clamp each end of large shapes; make sure all your clamps are positioned with their turnscrews on the same side of the fabric.

After tightening the clamps, soak the garment in water for about three minutes; then tighten the clamps again to prevent them from slipping. Holding the garment by the turnscrews, carefully lay it in a dyebath large enough to hold it without crowding. Lift sections of the garment occasionally to facilitate even penetration of the dye. When you like the color, rinse it out in warm water before you remove the clamps.

Any of the techniques described here can be combined on one garment. Do the dye work on the jacket first, and allow it to dry completely before painting on the felt. □

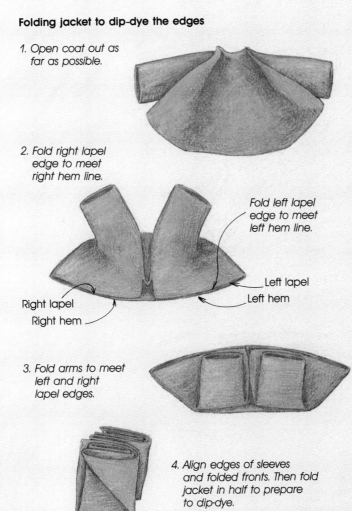

Folding jacket to dip-dye the edges

1. Open coat out as far as possible.

2. Fold right lapel edge to meet right hem line.

Fold left lapel edge to meet left hem line.

Right lapel
Right hem

Left lapel
Left hem

3. Fold arms to meet left and right lapel edges.

4. Align edges of sleeves and folded fronts. Then fold jacket in half to prepare to dip-dye.

Sources of Supply

Carded Wool Batting

Beau Monde
Rt. 30, Box 687
(N. Rupert)
Pawlet, VT 05761
(802) 325-3645
Brochure and newsletter $3.

Susan's Fiber Shop
N3967 O'Conner Rd.
Columbus, WI 53925
(414) 623-4237
Send SASE for price list.

Yolo Wool Products
Rt. 3, Box 171-D4
Woodland, CA 95695
(916) 756-7716
Sample catalog $2.

Dyes and pigments

Brooks & Flynn, Inc.
Box 2639
Rohnert Park, CA 94927-2639
(800) 822-2372
(in CA 800-345-2026)

Cerulean Blue
Box 21168
Seattle, WA 98111-3168
(206) 443-7744

PRO-Chemical & Dye, Inc.
Box 14
Somerset, MA 02726
(508) 676-3838

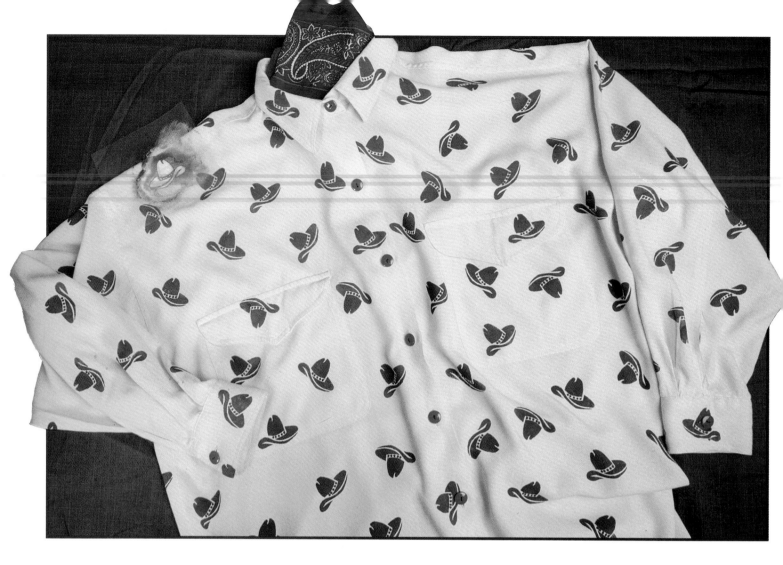

Sophisticated Stenciling
A simple way to print on fabric and clothing

by Diane Ericson

mention the word *stenciling,* and most people think of Early American interiors with stylized pineapples, eagles, and scrolling leaves repeated along the walls. It's a classic case of confusing a technique with a style. Apply modern materials and imagery to the process, and stenciling becomes one of the easiest techniques to explore and one of the most flexible methods for decorative surface design. It can be done on any flat surface, but I prefer to stencil on fabric. I've worked out many variations of the basic

technique, and I haven't looked at a piece of cloth or clothing in the same way since.

I use easy-to-cut acetate for stencil material and scraps of foam-rubber sponge to apply the fabric paint, and I can cut out a complex, subtle stencil and be printing in minutes. I've even transformed ready-to-wear, like the shirt in the photo above, with stencils, creating a new and unique garment in a few hours.

There are a number of sources for precut stencils and designs, but creating and cutting your own designs is so simple that precut ones are unnecessary. If you're protest-

ing that you can't draw and that you always work from predesigned patterns, relax. There are designs to trace everywhere, and not just from stencil books. Pictorial archives of stained-glass patterns, woodcuts, family crests and logos, historic and ethnic symbols, and letter forms are all wonderful resources for designs that easily translate into the flat shapes of stencil design, and they're just the tip of the iceberg. Strong designs

Using a hand-cut acetate stencil, fabric paint, and some red buttons, Diane Ericson transformed a plain yellow shirt into a unique garment.

From *Threads* magazine (May 1990) 28:68-73

can be made up of very simple shapes, and you can get great results with just one or two that you find pleasing. By masking, layering, and combining a few stencil images, you can produce an unlimited number of new images. I'll say more about designing later, but first I'll explain how I cut and use a simple stencil.

Making a stencil

The key to drawing (or tracing) a stencil is to keep in mind that you're drawing shapes, not lines. The shapes must be completely enclosed, ending at the point where you began. These enclosed shapes will be the holes that you cut out of the acetate and print through. You can darken in the shapes as you draw them; this will help you see the design as shapes instead of lines as you refine it. You can't have any nonprinting (negative) shapes floating unconnected within other shapes, because nonprinting areas are really the stencil material, and it has to be a single piece, no matter how complex. The connecting spaces (called bridges) are as important to your design as the spaces that you'll be printing, so take the time to design these areas as well. Traditional stencils tend to leave the same amount of space in between each cutout shape, but varying the shapes and amounts of that negative space can add much to a successful design.

For the stencil in the photos at right, I chose a simple Japanese knot shape and traced the outline on thin paper. I added a bit of contour to the lines that formed the bridges to suggest the folds in a knot of fabric. On top of the tracing I taped a piece of acetate about 2 in. bigger all around than my design. Acetate is measured by thickness; I use size .005 because it's neither so thin that it curls up and crinkles nor so thick that it makes printing difficult in the points and corners.

Next, I put the acetate/drawing layers on a cutting surface (I used a strip of heavy glass with smooth edges, but plastic matts, or even stacks of newspaper will work—curves can most easily be cut on glass) and cut them out with an X-Acto knife, going right through the paper underneath. I cut away the smallest details first, leaving more acetate to support the bigger cuts later. I started at the corners, as I always do, and cut away from them so that I wouldn't slip and cut beyond the corners. But don't worry if you do slip; it's very easy to repair the acetate. Just cover the cut on both sides with transparent tape, rub it down, and re-cut your shape.

The hip-pocket print shop

An incredible variety of results can be achieved with the stenciling process. The amount of paint you use and the color and

Ericson demonstrates printing with a simple stencil. With the stencil positioned on the fabric, she loads a foam sponge lightly with fabric paint, dabs it smooth on a plastic dish, and then starts dabbing through the acetate to cover the cloth more or less evenly. Printing unevenly (below), called grading, and printing through two stencils at a time, called layering, are among the techniques she uses to add texture and interest to the printed image. Before she moves the stencil, she can grade or print additional colors on top.

type of fabric you choose are only part of the story. There are also myriad ways to apply the paint through the stencil. Why not cut a few stencils and start experimenting?

You'll need the following tools and materials: A small bowl of water, two or three pieces of dense foam sponge, paper towels, fabric paints (I use Versatex and Createx, both widely available in lots of colors), a thick towel or rag, sticks or spoons for mixing paints, plastic container lids or plastic or paper plates for mixing in, sponge brushes (optional), and lots of small pieces of fabric in a variety of textures and colors to do the printing on. Spread your materials out on a clean, covered surface. If you're working with small images (up to 6 in.), you don't have to fasten the fabric to the table or the stencil to the fabric.

Rinse your foam sponge, and then squeeze out as much water as you can. Wrap the sponge in a towel and squeeze it again. When your sponge has just a hint of moisture in it, it's ready to use.

Stenciling takes very little paint and very little water. By using tiny amounts of paint and spending some extra time working it onto the surface of the fabric, I can get smooth, professional-looking results, and the fabric isn't stiff, even after layering on many colors. Spoon a small amount of the colors you'll be using along the edge of the palette, leaving most of the center free. Touch the sponge to the paint and dab it many times in a clean area until the paint

impression looks even. Next, holding the edges of the stencil gently on top of the fabric with your fingers, pat through the stencil lightly but firmly. After you've printed over the entire design, lift off the stencil.

For the sharpest images, work on smooth, finished fabrics. As a general rule, the smaller the details in your design, the finer the texture or weave of your fabrics should be if you want the details to show up when you're using subtle colors or gradations. As the texture of the fabric becomes coarser, it takes darker, heavier colors for the same delicate design to show up. If you want to print pastel, mix white directly into the color you'll use. However, if you want to print more vibrant light colors, you must do it in two stages. First, print the design with white paint in an even, thin coat. Allow that white to dry; then do a second application with the color on top. I find Versatex white better than Createx for this type of application; the Createx white seems to disappear into the fabric. Printing with white can also provide subtle variations on the color of your fabric. For example, if you're printing on a medium-green fabric, a first printing of white will produce a lighter green, and another layer after that will yield a very pale green.

Experiment with layers of different colors, working all the colors wet. Then try allowing them to dry between layers. Try printing with more water; the design will run together and be fuzzy when it dries. A

dry printing over a dried-out watery layer can produce wonderful effects.

Colorful, textural printing

Play with the following printing techniques as you develop your own style:

Grading is a method you can use to create a dimensional effect by printing more heavily in one area than in another. It's a good way to create emphasis in your design. Start by printing lightly all over the stencil. Then continue to print, concentrating in one area. This is a great technique for creating texture when you're printing with one color or with very subtle colors. When you're layering colors on top of one another, again remember to use small amounts of paint. If you want the colors to remain distinct, let them dry between applications. On the other hand, working colors wet creates softer effects and adds an element of spontaneity to the process.

Dry brush is the technique of brushing across the stencil with a foam sponge or sponge brush. You use the same amount of paint described above to create spontaneity and variation with one stencil. The stenciled design on the facing page was created with this technique.

Masking and layering are techniques you can use to expand your design options as your stencil collection grows. Even seemingly unrelated stencils have great potential in combination. To layer stencils, place one stencil over another and print right

Using the stencils to the left of the above design, Ericson created a natural, asymmetric, moving, and clustered design; with the stencils on the facing page, she created a formal, symmetrical, static, and orderly design.

through both as if they were one, as I did in the design on p. 43. Another way to get more from your stencil images is to mask them. This is especially effective when you want to stay with the feeling of your original design but don't want to continue printing the same image. First spend a few minutes looking at the stencil that you're using from different directions, perhaps covering sections with strips of paper. Look at the shapes, the amounts of printing area, and the similarities and differences among the shapes. My approach is to get rid of all hints of recognizable objects. I try to let go of the name of the original object and just see its characteristics. Names give us an efficient way to communicate, but they tend to make us stop looking at the thing we've named. As you explore the shapes, you may find a part of the design that looks worth printing as a new element, maybe in a different direction or flopped. Cut a window, the shape determined by the area you want to isolate, out of another piece of acetate, and place this window over your original stencil, taping it down in two or three places. This is how I evolved the design along the shoulder of the blouse in the photo on p. 46.

In addition to printing many colors through your stencil at one time, you may wish to create isolated areas of color by cutting separate stencils for each color. Once you've drawn your design, color it in before you start cutting. Then cut each color separately from its own piece of acetate. Print each piece one at a time, allowing each color to dry in between.

You may be creating unwanted texture by letting your fingernails press through the sponge as you print. If you have long nails, try wrapping your sponge in a bigger piece of the same foam, making a wad that will give a little more padding between your nails and the printing surface.

Creating designs

Nature is a wonderful source of ideas for patterning and placement: scattered leaves on a walk, stones arranged along the walkway, leaves braided together as they unfold from the center of a stalk. Man-made designs are also sources from which you can extract ideas: details on buildings; patterns on tiles, wallpaper, dishes, fabric.

For example, notice how things appear more three-dimensional when they create a shadow. Shadows can be explored easily through stenciling. Try printing a "shadow," first using your stencil in gray and then printing the same stencil a second time slightly off-center from the first one. Or cut a shadow stencil in a different shape. Notice how you can show a concept, like shapes hovering over the surface or shapes in different stages of taking off, indicating movement and direction of light, all using the shadow as a point of departure. What else do we live with every day that can be fuel for this process called designing?

Ask yourself how you respond to what you see. Do you prefer things that are clearly balanced or symmetrical? Or are you more drawn to things that are completely different on each side? Symmetrical arrangements are more stable, more conservative, and usually more formal. Asymmetry is more active; it indicates movement and is often more relaxed. Take time to feel which orientation you're most comfortable with. Perhaps you like asymmetry and formality or relaxed symmetry; the conflict could generate lots of energetic designs. Use your sample pieces to play with both types of arrangements as you practice and experiment with different printing techniques.

The design examples on these two pages illustrate both orientations in the creation of overall patterns. You should be able to start seeing some of the variety that's possible with just a few simple shapes (shown to the left of each design) and to begin recognizing basic design concepts, like scattering and clustering, borders, allover patterns, and directional patterning, which creates a feeling of movement.

One of the great advantages of stenciling is that you can place your patterns and design elements exactly where you want them. When I'm printing a garment that I'm mak-

Ericson extracted the abstract shapes along the shoulder of her self-designed blouse from the bird-on-a-branch design (background) by masking out parts of the original stencil.

ing, I cut out the pattern pieces first instead of printing yardage. This way, even if I'm going for an allover effect, I can still place repeating elements exactly as I want them, as I did on the collar points of the yellow shirt in the photo on p. 42. On a large table surface I lay out the cut fabric pieces as they'll go together (i.e., shoulders together and sleeves going out to the sides). Then I look at the relationship between the structural lines in the garment and the surface-design ideas I want to incorporate: Where do I want the emphasis? How do I want to direct attention to the piece when it's on the body? What kind of feeling do I want the piece to have?

Cleanup

After you've completed your printing, you must fix the paint on the fabric surface by a process of heat setting so the fabrics can be cleaned and washed. Read the setting procedure recommended for the paints you work with. Most will indicate ironing on the back or front with a press cloth, as hot as the fabric can handle, moving over each area for at least a minute with the iron. In general, fabrics with a high natural-fiber content hold the image better over time (and through washing) even if you apply paint in a more watery mix.

Your acetate stencils will last indefinitely if you take care of them. Clean them after each use by placing them in the sink under warm, running water. After a few minutes, rub them gently with your fingers. Most of the paints float off easily, and scrubbing isn't necessary. Pat them dry between absorbent paper or cloth towels.

My criterion for a storage system and access file for my stencil collection was that it should protect my stencils and also be an easy-to-use creative tool that would enhance my design process. My current system is working well; I keep the stencils in manila folders that I organize by categories: borders, plants, animals, geometrics, children's images, etc. I have a sheet of paper in between each of my stencils to keep them from hooking together and tearing as I take them out. As I design a new stencil, I print it once in black on a heavy sheet of white 8-in. x 11-in. stock (if the stencils are small, a lot of them fit on one sheet). This copy is a wonderful visual index of all the stencils I have. □

Diane Ericson designs and teaches in the Monterey Peninsula. She is the co-author with Lois Ericson of Design and Sew It Yourself: A Workbook for Creative Clothing *(1983), $19.95 + $1.50 P&H; and* Print It Yourself *(1980), $8.95 + $1.50 P&H. Both are available from Ericson at 650 Gibson Avenue, Pacific Grove, CA 93950.*

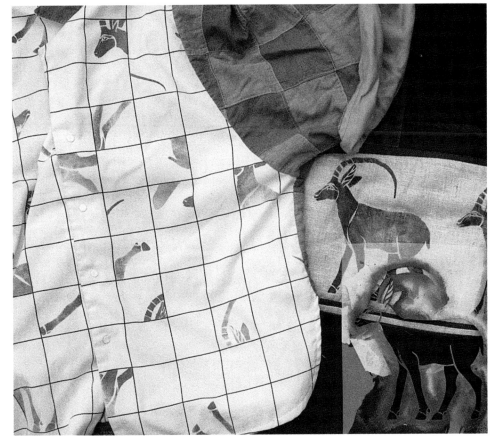

Selective masking from a natural image extracts multiple new designs that fit within the grid of commercially printed fabric. Antique fabric on the blouse of the ensemble below provided inspiration for rhythmically related stencils on the outer jacket.

The Embellished Vest

Techniques for making and decorating a fashion staple

by *Sandra Betzina*

Vests are always in fashion, in some form or another. Perhaps it's because they're almost more of an accessory than a piece of clothing. Textile embellishers and decorators have always regarded the vest as a perfect background for their efforts; the shape and construction are so simple that virtually all one's attention can be devoted to the surface treatment. I'll run through fitting and making a basic vest, and then I'll take a look at the tools and techniques I used on the vests at right that made embellishing them a simple process.

Fitting

The current look in vests is loose and oversize. You might want to buck the trend if you're petite and would be dwarfed by oversizing, but on many women a fitted vest will look skimpy these days. If you'd like your vest oversize, choose a man's vest pattern instead of trying to enlarge a woman's; the bust shaping on the woman's vest will get in your way. Try on vests from your husband's closet or the men's department of a local store, where you'll be able to check out a variety of sizes. For a woman size 8 to size 12, a men's medium (size 38) is a good place to start, both in patterns and trial garments.

After you've figured out the proportions you like, the only crucial area to fit on the vest is the shoulder, especially if you plan to wear it big and loose. You can pin-fit the pattern to determine shoulder adjustments, or simply allow 1-in. shoulder seam allowances when cutting out the vest so that you can alter the actual garment as you sew. In either case, pin the shoulder seam so that it fits the contour of your shoulder and the center front hangs perfectly vertical. If you prefer a well-fitted vest, make the same alterations on the vest pattern that you make on other garments.

Construction

Most vests are cut with a fashion fabric front and a lighter-weight lining fabric back. If the fashion fabric is not too heavy, I suggest you eliminate the front facings and either cut the fronts double, or line the vest to the edge. If you plan to pipe the outside edges of the vest, the piping will help keep the lining from rolling out at garment edges. Whatever you decide, make two separate vests, an outer and an inner layer. Complete all darts or princess seams and the shoulder seams on each one. Trim the shoulder seams on the inner layer to ¼ in. and on the outer layer to ½ in. Interface behind any styling details and the buttonholes on the outer layer. Complete any design details, such as collars, back belting, and front pockets, and attach them to the outer vest pieces.

Adding piping—Now's the time to make piping for the outside edges of your vest, if that's the look you want. Choose a fabric that will stand out and make the extra effort worthwhile. I look for stripes or fabric with a slight sheen or texture. Cut 2½-in.-wide bias strips, and join enough strips to go around the entire vest and both armholes, if you want piping there too.

San Francisco designer Kenneth King offers these tips for great-looking piping: For the filler, try rayon rattail cord, found in many trim departments and available by mail from Newark Dressmaker Supply (Box 2448, Lehigh Valley, PA 18001, 215-837-7500); it's much more flexible than cotton cording. Wrap your fabric around the cord and machine sew next to the rattail with a zipper foot. If you can adjust your needle position, move the needle as close as possible to the inside of the foot, away from the cording, as shown in the drawing at right. Now attach the piping to the right side of the outer layer only; sew along the matched seamlines with the needle slightly toward the outside of the zipper foot, closer to the piping. This way you'll be sewing completely inside the first stitching, and you'll stitch the piping to the garment as tightly as possible.

As you stitch the piping around corners and tight curves on the outer layer, ease the piping to the garment. If you stretch it, the piping won't lay flat when turned to the right side; it will twist to the front or back and look thin.

Joining the layers—If you're not adding piping, you need to make sure the inside layer stays neatly out of sight at the edges of the finished vest. Here's how: Trim ⅛ in. away from the inside layer at the armholes and all outside vest edges. (Don't trim the side seams, which should still be open on both layers.) If you align the raw edges of the inner and outer layers as you pin them together, the slightly smaller inner layer will pull the seamlines to the inside when the vest is turned right side out. If you're adding piping, skip this step.

Lay the outer vest right side up on your work surface and position the inner vest on top of it, wrong side up. Pin the two vests together at the armholes and around

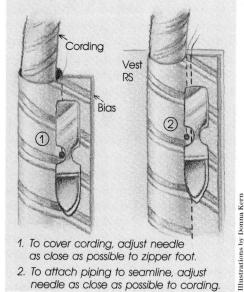

Adjusting needle positions for snug piping

1. To cover cording, adjust needle as close as possible to zipper foot.
2. To attach piping to seamline, adjust needle as close as possible to cording.

Illustrations by Donna Kern

From *Threads* magazine (July 1990) 29:50-53

Sandra Betzina's black vest (McCall's #4437) is made from waistband elastic seamed in strips into a flat fabric. The leather-bound vest (Burda #5278) is made from a single layer of double-faced cashmere, and the printed design is outlined here and there with rayon rattail cording, machine-stitched in lace with a Pearls 'n Piping foot. (Photo by Susan Kahn)

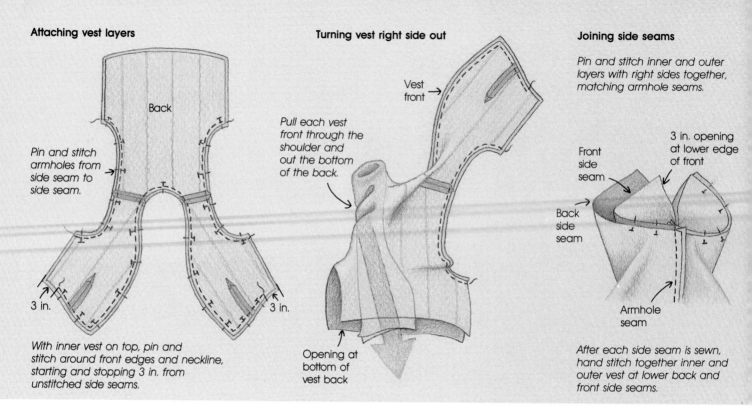

Attaching vest layers

Back

Pin and stitch armholes from side seam to side seam.

3 in.

3 in.

With inner vest on top, pin and stitch around front edges and neckline, starting and stopping 3 in. from unstitched side seams.

Turning vest right side out

Vest front

Pull each vest front through the shoulder and out the bottom of the back.

Opening at bottom of vest back

Joining side seams

Pin and stitch inner and outer layers with right sides together, matching armhole seams.

3 in. opening at lower edge of front

Front side seam

Back side seam

Armhole seam

After each side seam is sewn, hand stitch together inner and outer vest at lower back and front side seams.

the front edges, align the raw edges of the seam allowances, and match the shoulder seams. If you've added piping, it'll now be sandwiched between the layers. Starting 3 in. from the side seam along the lower front edge, pin up one side of the front, around the neckline, and down the other side, stopping 3 in. from the side seam on the opposite front, as shown above, left. Machine sew along this edge without going beyond the pins at either end, and then sew around each armhole. If there's piping involved, pin and sew with the outer layer on top, so that you can see the seamline of the attached piping and sew exactly on top of it. If there's no piping, sew with the inner layer up, so that the feed dogs will automatically assist you in easing the outer vest to the slightly smaller inner vest.

Clip all the curved seam allowances, especially that of the piping; I clip liberally at each curve and corner to within a single thread of the piping-to-garment stitching line. Then press the seams open, and grade and trim them. Turn the vest right side out by reaching from the back through the shoulder to each front and pulling each front out separately through the shoulder, as in the drawing above, center. Press, then pound all the seams flat with a tailor's clapper.

To close the side seams, pin the outer vest front and back side seams with right sides together, carefully matching the armhole seams, and continue across the seam to pin the front and back side seams of the inner vest, as shown above, right. Sew a continuous seam from outer vest to inner

vest in the same way for each side seam. Press the seams open, and trim away the bulk from the underarm seam joint. Now you can close the bottom of the vest by hand or partially machine-sew it by turning each side back on itself. Press and pound all outside edges well.

Decoration and trim

Both hand and machine techniques can provide beautiful results. Try needlepoint transfers, comics, and design books for pattern inspiration. Transfer designs to your fabric with Clo Chalk, a disappearing chalk, or vanishing-ink markers (both available from Clotilde, 1909 S.W. First Ave., Ft. Lauderdale, FL 33315-2100; 305-761-8655).

Machine work—Beading by machine is easy with a knit-edge foot, also known as a Pearls 'n Piping foot, a foot with a wide, deep channel down the center that was originally designed to absorb the loft when sewing bulky sweaters together. The channel under the foot allows the foot to ride over strung beads and other trims as you zigzag over them, as in the drawing on page 51. But the secret to invisible machine stitches in this process is to use a nearly invisible thread. The best I've found is called Invisible Wonder Thread, and it comes in clear for sewing on light colors and smoke for sewing on dark colors (available, like the foot, from Treadleart, 25834 Narbonne Ave, Lomita, CA 90717; 800-327-4222). This is not the wiry, scratchy, hard-to-control, see-through nylon thread we've all used, but a soft, transparent thread

almost as fine as a strand of hair and remarkably strong. It can be used in the bobbin as well as for the top thread. I used this foot-and-thread combo to attach the rattail trim that outlines selected shapes on the front of the paisley vest on p. 49.

To stitch over beads or rattail cord, use a 80/12 needle (H or Universal for wovens; HS or Ballpoint for knits). If your machine can be set to sew slowly and to stop with the needle down, do so; too high a speed might cause beads to catch in the foot, and the needle-down feature will hold your place as you arrange the trim or string of beads. Neither of these special machine capabilities are necessary—they just make the job easier.

Adjust your zigzag stitch width so that it clears the trim on either side and is long enough to go from bead to bead with every stitch. Fine-tune your adjustments on a scrap with a sample length of your trim or beading before you start on the actual project. If you break a needle more than once, switch to a size 90/14. On the final project, secure the first and last beads with a few zigzags set at 0 stitch length, and leave plenty of thread to tie off on the back.

Handwork—Authorities differ on the kind of thread to use for hand beading, but all agree that the cotton thread used in vintage garments has rotted. Cotton-wrapped polyester and silk thread are the most common recommendations for long life.

On both the vests in the photo on page 49, I've hand-applied beads, sequins, and

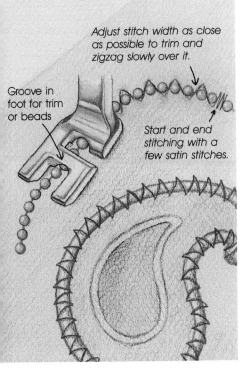

Pearls 'n Piping foot

Adjust stitch width as close as possible to trim and zigzag slowly over it.

Groove in foot for trim or beads

Start and end stitching with a few satin stitches.

Betzina attached each antique Japanese sequin to her waistband-fabric vest by hand, holding them in place with a tiny bead, front and back.

baubles, one at a time, either in rows (as on the black vest) or randomly (as on the paisley one). The technique is easy and decorative on both sides, as you can see in the detail photo above. I knot the thread and pull it through from the back, string on a sequin or large bead, and pick up a smaller bead—one that's bigger than the hole in the first object and complementary to it; then I go back through the first bead to the back. At the back I pick up another small bead and stitch back up under the large bead on the front, where I knot off. If I don't want a bead on the wrong side, I'll start with the first knot on the right side. For greater security, I sometimes put a dot of glue over the knots at the ends.

A leather-bound vest

You can add interest, save time, and cut down on seam bulk in your vest by finishing the edges with binding. You can bind two-layer vests, but the technique is ideal for fabrics that are thick enough to use in a single layer, like the double-faced cashmere I used for my paisley vest. I like to use leather binding because you don't have to worry about raw edges and because it's so beautiful. You don't need an industrial machine to sew on light- to medium-weight suedes or leathers. Just put a leather sewing machine needle (NTW or wedge) and an even-feed or Teflon foot (so the leather doesn't drag against the foot) on your machine, and choose a leather that's about the weight and thickness of Ultrasuede, and you'll

have no problem. Of course, you can choose a synthetic for your binding if you prefer it or if you want your vest to be washable; use an 80/12 (HS/Ballpoint) needle and either of the feet recommended above on synthetics.

Normally you'd trim off the seam allowances from the edges that you intend to bind. But before you trim, try on the vest to see if you'll like the proportions better with the allowances left on; they'll make the armholes smaller and the edges longer, which might improve the look of an oversize garment.

If you're using a synthetic leather, cut the binding strips in the direction of greatest flexibility: crosswise or well off-grain. Cut genuine leather binding strips wherever you can get the longest strips. For a ⁵⁄₈ in. or narrower binding, cut the strips 2½ in. wide and join them to form a strip long enough to go around the entire vest, including armholes.

To construct a bound vest, whether it's one or two layers, simply join fronts and backs at the shoulder and side seams. If your vest is two layers, arrange the completed layers wrong sides together, and hand- or machine-baste lining and vest together along outside and armhole edges.

Unless you're adept at mitering, round off all the corners of the vest slightly; it'll make attaching the binding easier. Place the right side of the binding against the right side of the vest, with raw edges matching. Try to position seams on the strip in the least-visible areas, such as underarms and the back of the neck. Ma-

chine-sew the binding to the garment with ⁵⁄₈-in. seams. If you want narrower binding, carefully trim the raw edges now; I usually trim them to ³⁄₈ in. Clip all the curves in the seam allowances, and wrap the raw edge of the fabric with the wide side of the binding. Pin the binding in place from the right side of the vest, and working right side up, machine sew it in place by stitching in the ditch. On the wrong side, trim away any excess binding outside the stitching line.

A vest from waistband elastic

My black vest was made from nine yards of ruffled-edge waistband material, which I found when I was rummaging around in a fabric store. I joined strips together to create a fabric surface from which I cut the vest fronts, cutting the strips 2 in. longer than the approximate width I needed for the various sections of the vest. I topstitched the ruffled edge of the elastic onto the flat edge of the next piece of elastic, stitching each row from the center out to each end, which helped prevent stretching of the elastic. With such a stiff and irregular fabric, I had to limit styling details to darts and false pocket flaps, but I had no trouble adding piping and a collar in rayon ottoman fabric.

Sandra Betzina's latest book, More Power Sewing, Master's Techniques of the 21st Century, is available for $19.95 plus $3 postage in U.S. or $5 in Canada from Power Sewing, Dept. B, 185 Fifth Ave., San Francisco, CA 94118.

...from Threads magazine   51

Clothes to Live In

Clean finish, elegant detailing, and sturdiness, in one flat-fell swoop

by Jeanne Engelhart

i design clothes that I hope will remind people that life is meant to be enjoyed and fulfilling, not overstuffed with struggle and discomfort. When you put on an interesting outfit that makes you feel easy and light, you are declaring these qualities a priority in your life. They are for me, and that's why I got into this business. (See "Angelheart takes flight" on p. 54 for more about that).

I learned by the seat of my pants. After graduating from college, my twin sister and I taught ourselves how to sew because we were uninspired by available fashions. I had no formal training in clothing design or sewing and I think this was advantageous. I wasn't locked into what I "could" or "shouldn't" do. I explored concepts in construction and design that maybe weren't "acceptable." I didn't know any better and it worked.

Washable, wearable fabrics

For my warm weather fabric I use a washed linen. There is nothing like linen. It's cool, and the more it's washed the less wrinkles there are. It's actually the oils in linen that keep it stiff and make it wrinkle. As the oils get washed out, the linen gets more relaxed and comfortable. We take it to the local laundry to be washed and put through the mangles. Then it's ready to use and it sews up beautifully.

We distinguish our linens by silkscreening them right here in our barn. We print the separate pieces of the garment, after it is cut, before sewing. We aren't printing the scrap fabric and can position the de-

Comfort, fun, and ease of wear are the hallmarks of Angelheart designs. Begin with the fabrics: washed linen and cotton double knits. Cut generously and simply. Then add functional detail—flat-fell seams in many guises. (Photo by William McDowell)

From *Threads* magazine (January 1991) 32:30-35

sign in relation to the garment pieces.

For fall and winter, I use a reversible, cotton double knit, which I'm able to design myself. I draw the pattern and choose my colors, weight, and texture. It is knit up for me by New York Fabrics (39 W. 37th St., New York, NY 10018) exactly to my specifications. The minimum order is 2500 yds., in two colorways. This autumn my knit fabric was inspired by the fall foliage. I superimposed an art deco motif onto the leaves, creating something very contemporary and unique (photo, left). The opposite side is a heathery solid giving a totally different option.

For spring, I work with linens, which I get from Hamilton-Adams Imports (PO Box 2489, 101 Country Ave., Secaucas NJ 07094). They come in a wonderful range of solid colors. I chose two groups: raspberry, teal, deep periwinkle and an autumn-jungle maize, burnt orange, moroccan brown, khaki, lime green.

Designing for comfort and fun

It's quite fascinating where you can get ideas from if you keep your eyes, and, more importantly, your mind, open. I'm always looking for tips, be they from nature, an interesting cabinet door, or an old flight suit. I watch people, how clothes fall on them, what shapes work, and which ones don't. I watch children, toddlers; what do they seem to be at ease in? I am definitely influenced by children's clothes of the '20s, '30s, and '40s; designs for kids were done with comfort and fun in mind. Details, too, were much more interesting in the past.

Styles—When I start to design, I am ultimately designing for myself. I only make clothes that I will love to wear. I design big. If there is a lot of fabric around you, you look smaller and feel more comfortable. I like the clothes to hang down straight, not touching the body at all, leaving room for the imagination. ⇨

The Market coat (above) is based on the cover-up smock. It makes a great duster, and by varying the hemline and fullness at back, Engelhart has created some wonderful jackets, as well. One of the first garments Engelhart made was button-up pants, with low crotch, roomy hip, and elastic back waist. The latest version (below) is in linen, of course. (Photos by William McDowell)

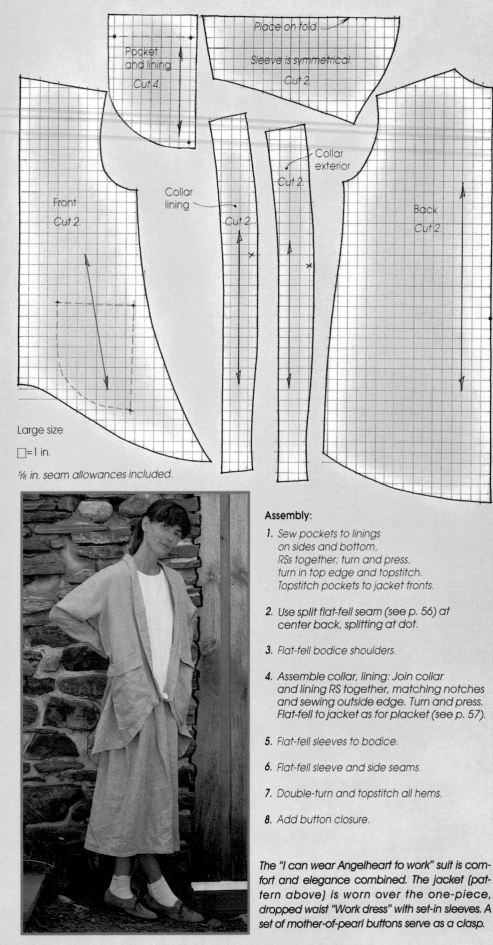

Pocket and lining Cut 4.

Place on fold.

Sleeve is symmetrical. Cut 2.

Front Cut 2.

Collar lining

Collar exterior Cut 2.

Cut 2.

Back Cut 2.

Large size

□=1 in.

⅝ in. seam allowances included.

Assembly:

1. Sew pockets to linings on sides and bottom, RSs together; turn and press, turn in top edge and topstitch. Topstitch pockets to jacket fronts.

2. Use split flat-fell seam (see p. 56) at center back, splitting at dot.

3. Flat-fell bodice shoulders.

4. Assemble collar, lining: Join collar and lining RS together, matching notches and sewing outside edge. Turn and press. Flat-fell to jacket as for placket (see p. 57).

5. Flat-fell sleeves to bodice.

6. Flat-fell sleeve and side seams.

7. Double-turn and topstitch all hems.

8. Add button closure.

The "I can wear Angelheart to work" suit is comfort and elegance combined. The jacket (pattern above) is worn over the one-piece, dropped waist "Work dress" with set-in sleeves. A set of mother-of-pearl buttons serve as a clasp.

Angelheart takes flight

It would be ludicrous to design and manufacture clothing that expresses lightheartedness and not create a happy work place. I cross the driveway every morning to orchestrate the production of thousands of garments, to manage the activities of 15 Angelbees and hundreds of thousands of dollars with the same question in mind: How do I make it all happen and at the day's end have love, abundance, and gratitude clearly in the lead, with fear and lack high-tailing it out of town?

For me this journey began in February of 1987, when I took a break from carpentry and accompanied Jeanne to our first wholesale show. We wrote $17,000 worth of orders. My triumphant bliss was soon deflated; while in the hotel pool relaxing after a day of selling, I asked my beloved how she had come up with her wholesale prices. As we went through the breakdown of each garment the news was similar; our profit would be about two dollars a garment. We had gone the route of many by initially underselling ourselves. Chalk it up to advertising.

That June I pushed Jeanne into going to New York to attend the International Fashion and Boutique Show with a fall line. Knowing only linen, we used it. I dyed the sample yardage (purple, pumpkin, evergreen, and periwinkle) in the backyard in our 40 quart tofu pots. After taking $40,000 worth of orders, we traipsed around Brooklyn looking for a dyer, who we paid $5,000 up front with no idea how we could cover the check. On our return there was a notice for an opening at the Lincoln Center Craft Fair. That weekend we sold $10,000 of retail Angelheart and stayed afloat. The following January we moved into 900 square feet of renovated space in our barn, liberating our living room. Next we added an inventory room, packing room, and finally an office.

I can't impart much more business sense upon my readers; I have none. I have never seen a cash flow chart, don't know what my overhead is or make any decisions based on the state of the economy. I choose to think that innocence and imagination are more powerful than reason. I'm often asked why our clothes are expensive (dresses wholesale around $170, pants around $110, and coats around $200). "They're sewn by people with mortgages and car payments," is my standard reply.

—Matthew Engelhart

The first season I made a pair of comfy, hip-hiding baggy pants, with a long crotch, elastic in the back waist, and roomy pockets. A more refined version, the "Button-up pants," (bottom photo, p. 53) is still in the line. So is the "Market coat" (top photo, p. 53), one of my favorite pieces. I was wearing one of my father's old work coats (he runs the Hunt's Point Produce Market) to protect my clothes, and caught sight of myself in the mirror. It looked great. Its loose, easy shape is also the basis of the shorter jackets we do.

Intuitive draping—So I get an idea and madly sew it up, usually using parts from passé or rejected pieces that are hanging around. Perhaps I'll make the bottom of a dress from an old skirt and the sleeves from some jacket. I do this because I'm too impatient to sew it all up from scratch, but I've discovered little surprises this way that I incorporate into the final garment. Let's say I am sewing up a front piece to a different, shorter back. I add a small piece to give it the length, and lo and behold, it's an interesting detail and so it remains.

When I've come up with a very rough finished piece, I put it on and look and look and look and look and if I'm not satisfied I pull it up here, push it out there, put it on backwards, inside out, and even upside down if I can, all the time looking and looking. Sometimes it works right away. Other times I play with the piece until something catches my eye. Something says yes, whether it be a neckline or the shoulder or the placement of a seam or pocket, and I go from there. What is the feeling of this component and why do I like it? How do I let it flow through the whole piece? What type of sleeves feel like that? What type of bodice? How about the skirt, shall it be pleated? Straight? I guess you'd call this draping.

My patternmaker, Diana Skawold, asked me at the beginning of our relationship if I designed by draping or flat pattern method. I honestly had no idea what she was talking about. So after I'm finished "draping," Diana comes in and does her miracle work.

After five seasons I am still very impressed. I can hand her something partially sewn, partially pinned, basically glued together by intention. I describe the impulse behind it and she creates the pattern for that dream. We fine-tune the piece by making alterations. We usually end up sewing a piece three to six times before it goes into production. We do get the occasional grueller which we tinker with even after we've started manufacturing it. We've also experienced the satisfaction in finding it just right on our first attempt. This is my designing process. Diana has certainly helped make it smoother and more enjoyable, and added a professional dimension

where it was sorely needed. You should have seen some of the patterns when it was my job. The sewers always needed to trim pieces so they would fit together, making each garment "unique."

Construction: no fuss, no muss
No, patternmaking was not my forte. However, I have cooked up a few cockamamie ideas about sizing, cutting, sewing, and pattern shapes that we have maintained.

Sizing—I like loose, comfortable clothing and I refuse to be a size medium. So you could say the whole sizing system is based on my vanity. I am the small (I weigh between 120 and 125) and we go up and down from there, usually grading 3 in. to 4 in. per size. The chart turns out to be: 4-6 petite, 8-10 small, 12-14 medium, 16-18 large, with room to spare, of course!

Cutting out—After grading our paper patterns (which we file away) and making a sample in each size, we cut our working patterns out of heavy flannel chamois, including a ⅝-in. seam allowance. The edges are all outlined with black marker that will be noticed if it gets trimmed off during cutting. The flannel is fairly heavy and sticks to the fabric, so no pins or weights are needed. These patterns are much easier to fold up than paper, they last, and they store well. We've recently purchased a heavy-duty rotary cutter (from Maimin Co. Inc., Kent, CT) that goes through layers of fabric like butter.

Pattern pieces—I like to simplify cutting as much as possible. For collars and plackets, for instance, we have one pattern for all sizes and it's long enough to accommodate a large size. We sew them on (see drawing on p. 57), positioning one edge, then sewing toward the other. When we're close to the end, we trim it to length, and finish.

I nearly always use the same sleeve pattern for all sizes. What!? Yes, I do and it makes cutting more efficient. If we cut too many, they'll be okay for any size. Furthermore, my sleeves are symmetrical. Sleeves can be cut on the fold if necessary, and for

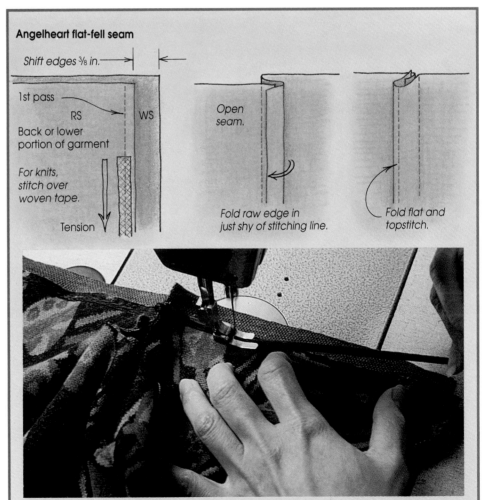

Angelheart flat-fell seam

Shift edges ⅜ in.

1st pass

RS   WS

Back or lower portion of garment

For knits, stitch over woven tape.

Tension

Open seam.

Fold raw edge in just shy of stitching line.

Fold flat and topstitch.

Flat-felled seams in knits with a straight-stitch machine? Yes, with the aid of narrow woven tape. Center the tape over the first seamline, and with presser foot and needle down, pull firmly but gently on the tape as you let the knit feed naturally. Practice a bit; soon your seam will be stable, without puckers or unwanted curves.

the reversible or printed fabric it's great.

You never end up with two left sleeves nor 20 for that matter. The seamstress doesn't need to take extra time figuring out which is the front. My clothes are built simply and roomy enough that this concept "eases in" beautifully. The sewers like that. And without my sewers, who all do a wonderful job transforming my visions into reality, this business would not be.

Stitching—While designing I think of the production and how difficult or simple a concept will be to sew. A piece isn't successful in my mind unless it comes together really easily for the sewer. Therefore I am constantly working on elements that look intricate but actually are sewn up quite quickly and smoothly. It's fun; it's like figuring out a puzzle. In the process I've come up with some innovative techniques in clothing construction.

Take flat-felled seams, for instance. They're not so innovative in themselves, although I don't know of another clothing line which is completely manufactured that way. In my flat-felled seams, rather than worrying about two different seam allowances or having to trim the allowance after the first pass, we simply shift the fabric to offset the edges by ⅜ in., then sew, fold (finger-pressing the linen), and topstitch (see drawing, p. 55).

I love the clean, finished seam you get both inside and out. In fact, I have made a reversible line based on this concept, using the double-faced cotton knits. It was an excellent medium for the flat-fell seam except for one major drawback. The seams stretch when you sew with knits. I don't have overlock machines. I don't even like the look of serged seams, which would put an end to the reversibility. We sew a narrow (¼ in.) woven cotton edge tape along the inside edge of the flat-fell seam on the first pass. It works great; it just takes a little practice. The sewers keep a slight tension on the tape while they allow the knit to feed through naturally (photo, p. 55). When the second pass of stitching is finished, the tape is hidden in a nice firm seam. For more on using flat-felled seams, see the box at right.

As you sew, join me in a life where we allow ourselves to laugh often, have fun, have a ball! Where we don't take ourselves so seriously. Remember, angels fly because they take themselves lightly. ☐

Jeanne Engelhart and her husband, Matthew, make and market functional, comfortable clothes under the name Angelheart Designs. For more information and a catalog, write to them at 303 Gunderman Rd., Spencer, NY 14883.

Making a virtue of necessity— variations on a flat-fell seam

One of the pieces of my construction puzzle has its roots as much in efficiency as in style. I want a smoothly finished garment, with no raw edges, no hemstitching, no finicky work. So I plan each garment as an assembly of variations on a flat-fell seam (drawing, p. 55). From inserting sleeves to hemming, the finish and the detail are one and the same.

SPLIT SEAM—*This is great for sewing a side seam and armhole finish in one (photo, above left). It's also an effective detail for a center-front to neck opening transition. The simple slit with buttonloop is constructed the same way as is the deep V with inset (above right), except that the reverse side of the seam acts as the face, as shown in the drawing below.*

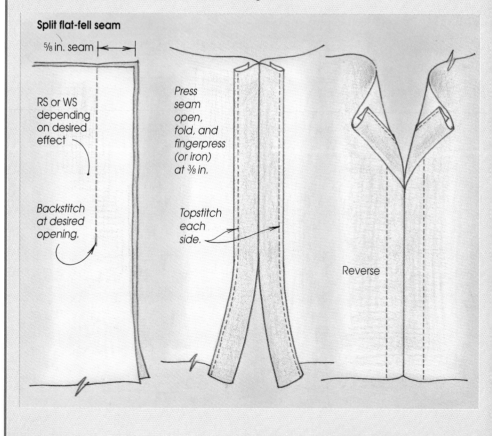

Split flat-fell seam

⅝ in. seam

RS or WS depending on desired effect

Backstitch at desired opening.

Press seam open, fold, and fingerpress (or iron) at ⅜ in.

Topstitch each side.

Reverse

PLACKETS—Here we maintain the look by attaching the placket to the shirt or jacket front with a flat-fell seam. We cut the placket extra long, then fold it lengthwise and topstitch top and visible edge. Then we "flat-fell" placket to bodice as shown in the drawing at right.

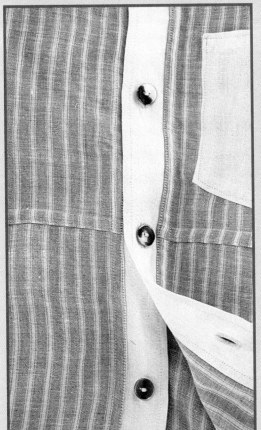

Placket

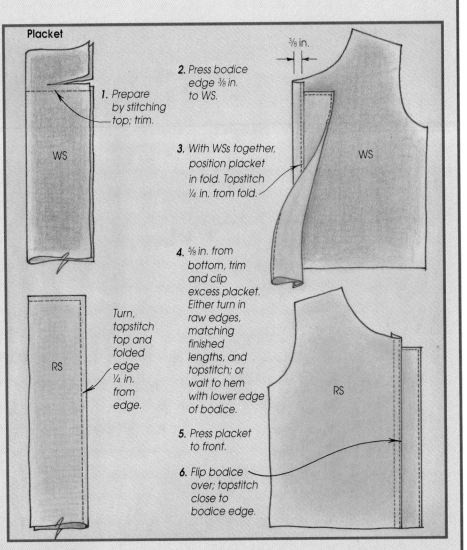

1. Prepare by stitching top; trim.

WS

RS

Turn, topstitch top and folded edge ¼ in. from edge.

⅜ in.

2. Press bodice edge ⅜ in. to WS.

3. With WSs together, position placket in fold. Topstitch ¼ in. from fold.

WS

4. ⅝ in. from bottom, trim and clip excess placket. Either turn in raw edges, matching finished lengths, and topstitch; or wait to hem with lower edge of bodice.

5. Press placket to front.

6. Flip bodice over; topstitch close to bodice edge.

RS

SLEEVES—This sleeve, cut with the seam at the shoulder rather than the underarm, is flat-felled to the side-seamed bodice. Then shoulder and sleeve seam are flat-felled as one. —J.E.

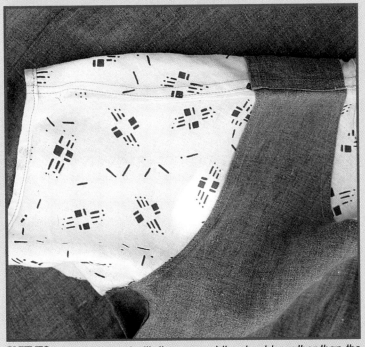

POCKETS—The opening edges of these pockets are finished with a topstitched double turn that echoes the flat-fell seam. The remaining edges of the pockets are sewn into the flat-fell seams that join the pieces.

Sew Yourself a Sweater

Sewing machine solutions for handling textured knit yardage

by Connie Long

making beautiful sweaters and knit jackets is not just for knitters. Almost all of the sweaters that are manufactured in the United States are cut and stitched from sweater bodies, lengths of knit fabric with a knit-in ribbed bottom. Machine knitters often knit yardage, and then just sew a sweater together. You can sew yourself an entire wardrobe of wonderful sweaters using only fabric sold by the yard. I am always coming upon new sweaterknits to play with, knits that are richly textured with dimensional stitches, jacquard designs, lacey pointelles, cables, or tweeds.

If a matching rib trim is unavailable, don't worry. There are other ways to finish the neckline, hem, or edges with readily available materials such as lightweight UltraSuede (Facile), jersey, or self-fabric. I'll discuss finishing techniques after giving guidelines for pattern selection and modification, and sewing.

The sweater at left was made without knitting needles. Using a pattern meant for wovens, author Connie Long cut knit yardage, stitched the garment together, and trimmed edges with jersey. (Photos by Yvonne Taylor)

Knits with body

I apply the term "sweaterknits" to fabrics that are textured and usually heavier than jersey or doubleknit; they are also called novelty knits. Sweaterknits come in widths from 36 in. to 60 in., and in natural and synthetic fibers. Most stores don't carry them throughout the year, but I often find one or two in season.

If you're going to make an open garment like a cardigan or jacket, and the wrong side of the knit may show, or if you're trying to find a coordinating trim, check the wrong side of the fabric. The reverse of a floral or geometric jacquard knit often has a stripe or tweedy pattern, which would complement the right side if applied as a binding. Sometimes the difference in stitch or texture from right to wrong side provides a good coordinating trim.

While you're considering a sweaterknit, and if a matching rib is not in sight, look for a jersey in the same color as the sweaterknit or a matching Facile. Because of boiled wool's popularity in recent years, fabric stores have a good selection of fold-over trims that also work beautifully with all types of knits. Chanel-type braids are another possibility. If the sweaterknit can be raveled, you can even knit your own ribbing from the yarn.

Before cutting any sweaterknit or buying yardage, test a swatch for shrinkage, particularly if you question the fiber content. Measure the swatch, then gently hand wash and lay it flat to dry on a towel. I've found that cottons are more likely to shrink than wools. Cottons can be gently machine washed and dried to shrink them as much as possible prior to cutting. Cottons never really stop shrinking. After they are sewn together, it's best to air dry them. The white cabled knit fabric of the jacket shown on the facing page is pure wool and the swatch shrank very little. After hand washing the yardage with baby shampoo and no agitation, I laid it on a towel-covered bed to dry flat.

Check if the manufacturer's fold is still visible after washing; if so, you'll have to work around it when you cut out the pieces.

Keep it simple

Patterns meant specifically for knits are available from every major pattern source. However, check the pattern's seam allowances; a ¼-in. seam allowance that is appropriate for thin jersey or doubleknit is too narrow for thick sweaterknits, which have looser and larger stitches and tend to ravel and distort. For best results, always plan to use ½-in. or wider seam allowances; you can trim them to ¼ in. after stitching the seam twice.

If your knit is fairly stable, you can select a more dramatic look by using a pattern meant for woven fabric. Look for simple lines. Horizontal lines translate poorly into sweaterknits because the seams stretch and ripple.

Sweaters tend to grow, so when using a pattern meant for a woven fabric, you can usually use a size smaller with sweaterknits. Check the pattern dimensions first. I like roomy garments, so I often use my regular size unless the pattern is very oversized.

A conventional "for wovens" pattern made with a knit will often require less yardage because you can eliminate facings and hem allowances, and bind the edges. In fact, you can often eliminate seams, and should eliminate darts. Since a knit has much greater stretch than a woven, structure doesn't have to be sewn into the garment.

The white sweatercoat is a soft version of my favorite ¾-length wrap coat; the oversized pattern with simple lines is for wovens. I was able to eliminate the center-back seam by placing the pattern on a fold, but the dolman sleeves, too wide for the amount of fabric I had, had to be pieced.

The pattern I started with for the waist-length blue jacket shown at right is for wovens; it has front and collar facings, darts in the back and front, side seams, and a center-back collar seam. Otherwise, the pattern is simple enough.

To modify it for a reversible sweaterknit that has a checkerboard pattern of knit and purl, I eliminated the facings since the collar and lapels could be turned back in the reversible fabric (top drawing, right). I decided to turn the collar's center-back seam into a decorative element. The darts were folded out of the pattern; for the pattern pieces to lie flat, the darts had to be folded past their actual length. This does not cause fitting problems; the knit expands to accommodate the bust. In eliminating the side seams, I also straightened the jacket's taper by overlapping the sewing lines at the armhole but spreading them ½ in. at the hem. The sleeve pattern was fine except that the cap had too much ease for a sweaterknit; I removed the ease by redrawing the cap flatter.

When laying out the pattern, use pattern weights if you find that pins tear the paper. Another technique is to trace the pattern with white tailors' chalk on colored fabrics or with disappearing-ink pen on white.

Seams

The familiar phrase "stretch and sew" does not apply to sewing most sweaterknit seams, which, due to the fabric's thickness, tend to stretch anyway. The sewing machine's foot and feed dog squeeze the thick layers together and spread the fabric outward from the needle. To counteract

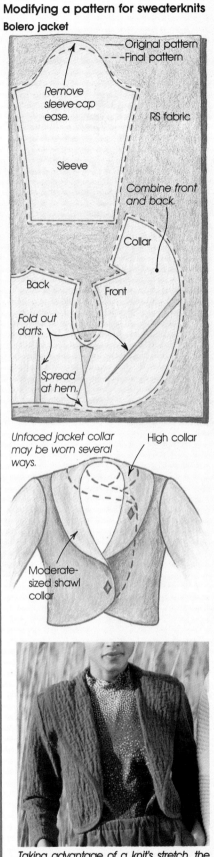

Modifying a pattern for sweaterknits
Bolero jacket

— Original pattern
-- Final pattern

Remove sleeve-cap ease.

RS fabric

Sleeve

Combine front and back.

Collar

Back

Front

Fold out darts.

Spread at hem.

Unfaced jacket collar may be worn several ways.

High collar

Moderate-sized shawl collar

Taking advantage of a knit's stretch, the author made this bolero without side seams, facings, or darts (top drawing). The edges, bound and trimmed with Facile, are as neat on the inside as the outside.

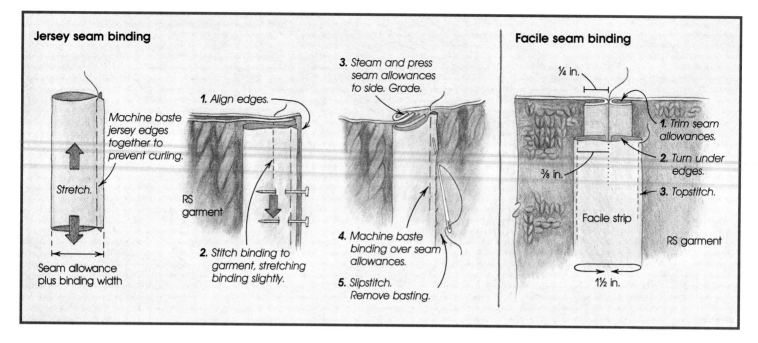

Jersey seam binding

Machine baste jersey edges together to prevent curling.

Stretch.

Seam allowance plus binding width

1. Align edges.

RS garment

2. Stitch binding to garment, stretching binding slightly.

3. Steam and press seam allowances to side. Grade.

4. Machine baste binding over seam allowances.

5. Slipstitch. Remove basting.

Facile seam binding

¼ in.

⅜ in.

Facile strip

1½ in.

1. Trim seam allowances.

2. Turn under edges.

3. Topstitch.

RS garment

---

the spread and distortion, use fewer stitches and help the fabric feed into the needle.

Start with good quality polyester thread for stretch and set the stitch length longer than normal, approximately 10 to 14 stitches per inch. A universal needle and straight stitches are fine for stable sweaterknits, although you can try zigzag or stretch stitches too. Don't pull on the fabric; push it into the foot as you stitch. If the seam still looks like it's stretching, decrease the number of stitches per inch. For very thick knits, you may need to try an even-feed foot or a roller foot (see *Basics, Threads,* No. 36, pp. 16 and 18), available from sewing machine dealers or mail-order notions companies, that will help feed the fabric layers into the needle.

If you're using a serger and the stitching is stretching the seam, adjust the differential feed and the number of stitches to a position that would usually gather thinner fabrics.

Elastic stay—Horizontal seams need to be stayed because they distort more than vertical ones. However, if a seam, like the shoulder, is stayed too tightly, the knit stretches immediately around it while the restricted seam remains rigidly in shape; the end of the seam where it meets the sleeve pulls the sleeve cap to a point. I believe in letting the seam stretch to some extent because that's its nature, so I stay the seam with thin ¼-in.- or ⅜-in.-wide elastic.

Sew the shoulder seams with straight or stretch stitches, then position the elastic in the seam allowance ⅛ in. over the seamline. You can leave the elastic uncut and use exactly what you need, trimming it after stitching. Stretch the elastic just a little and zigzag in place; the innermost edge of the zigzag should be on the seamline.

The correct amount of stretch slightly curls up the seam ends without making the seam shorter or gathered.

Seam binding—One challenge of making a sweater jacket is seam treatment. A technique that stabilizes seams, hides seam allowances, and enhances the design is sewing seams wrong sides together and then binding them on the right side of the garment. You can buy knit binding, but making binding from yardage lets you choose the width.

I decided that the smooth texture of white jersey would work well with the clean lines and texture of the white cabled knit; see the left drawing above. I also noted that fabric pieces with different grainlines converge and could look too busy in such a directional knit; the jersey would frame each area and define it. In contrast, the dressy suedelike texture of Facile seemed suitable paired with the blue sweaterknit (right drawing above).

Taming the great expanse

One thing you quickly learn when working with sweaterknits is that they can expand on the crossgrain. Before you can finish edges on hems, collars, and sleeve openings with binding, you need to restore them to their original length. The cables of the white sweater, for example, fanned out. To preserve the original tapered shape and to control the accordion effect, I stayed the edges.

Using the pattern as a guide, measure and cut lengths of preshrunk rayon seam binding or twill tape the same length as the edges. Rayon seam binding is softer and easier to shape than polyester. Preshrink rayon by submerging it in hot water, squeezing out excess, and ironing it dry. Mark the tape length at the center-back and side seams so when you match the tape to the

edge, you can distribute the ease of the knit evenly. Pin the tape to the garment edge within the seam allowance and next to the seamline. With the tape on top, machine stitch the tape to the garment, close to the seamline. The seam binding or twill tape should be positioned so that it will be enclosed by the binding and be invisible.

No-muss edge trim

Facile makes a nice trim because it is thin and doesn't ravel, but it has limited stretch on the crossgrain, unlike bias tape that has a lot of stretch. This means a Facile trim for an inside curved edge, such as a neckline, must be kept narrow and be stretched as much as possible, or it will bunch and wrinkle. Facile is not stretched at all for trimming outside curves. For most garments, an eighth-yard of Facile provides plenty of trim.

Cut Facile strips approximately 2 in. wide and, if necessary, piece to get the length of the neckline or edge plus two seam allowances. You can sew the strips with right sides together and finger press the seams open. Or you can overlap and topstitch along the seamlines, and trim the top seam allowance close to the stitches.

Divide the garment edge and the trim into quarters. Position the trim on the garment with right sides together, matching the quarter marks and pinning only in the seam allowances. For inside curves, stretch the Facile as you pin and use a narrow ½-in. seam allowance. Sew outside curves with a ⅝-in. seam allowance. Finger press the trim up and around the raw edge and the rayon stay tape. From the right side, pin in the well of the seam to secure the Facile edge on the wrong side and, if necessary, baste. Make sure the binding looks even, then topstitch the Facile close to the fold or in the well of

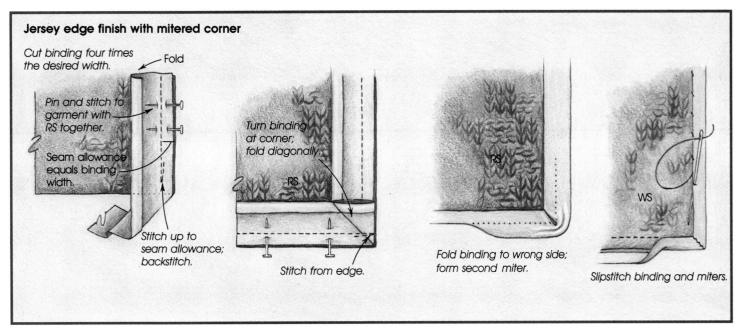

Jersey edge finish with mitered corner

Cut binding four times the desired width.

Fold

Pin and stitch to garment with RS together.

Seam allowance equals binding width.

Stitch up to seam allowance; backstitch.

Stitch from edge.

Turn binding at corner; fold diagonally.

RS

RS

Fold binding to wrong side; form second miter.

WS

Slipstitch binding and miters.

---

the seam. (When both sides need to look the same, as in my blue jacket, topstitch so the stitching catches the Facile on both the front and the back; trim excess Facile close to the topstitching on the back.

You can also use jersey to trim edges, as shown in the drawing sequence above.

Unribbed rib

When matching ribbing for cuffs, neckline, or waistbands is simply not available, strips of knits with limited stretch such as jersey, doubleknit, cotton interlock, or self-fabric can work just as well. The trick is to stretch the edge that attaches to the garment so the curved trim lies flat against your body (drawing sequence, right).

Cut a strip of jersey or doubleknit on the crossgrain, twice the desired finished width plus two seam allowances and longer than the neckline or edge. Fold it in half lengthwise and machine baste, stretching the fabric as much as possible. Compare it to the curve of the garment edge to see if it follows that line and lies flat. Usually it will. Cut the stretched band equal to the edge length plus two seam allowances. With right sides together, sew the ends of the band together to form a closed circle.

Sew the band to the garment with right sides together, proceeding as if you were working with ribbing, dividing the band and neckline into quarters to distribute the trim equally. When using this trim for close-fitting necklines (crew neck) or tapered openings like cuffs, make sure the edge trim fits over your head or hands as well as into the garment opening. □

Connie Long, a designer and sewing instructor from Mitchellville, MD, wrote about working with lace in Threads, *No. 29.*

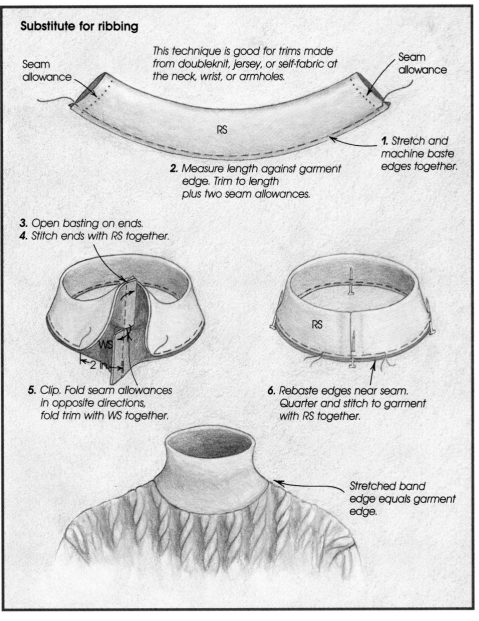

Substitute for ribbing

Seam allowance

This technique is good for trims made from doubleknit, jersey, or self-fabric at the neck, wrist, or armholes.

Seam allowance

RS

1. Stretch and machine baste edges together.

2. Measure length against garment edge. Trim to length plus two seam allowances.

3. Open basting on ends.
4. Stitch ends with RS together.

WS

2 in.

5. Clip. Fold seam allowances in opposite directions, fold trim with WS together.

RS

6. Rebaste edges near seam. Quarter and stitch to garment with RS together.

Stretched band edge equals garment edge.

Jeans and slacks compared
Jeans: Navy line ——
Slacks: Gold line ——

Who Needs Calvin Klein?

How to draft and construct
a pair of authentic jeans

by Jerry Sider

i had been looking for a week and finally found them: burgundy denim bell-bottoms. But my visit to the fitting room was a flop; I returned the pants to the salesclerk. I was walking away when he asked, "What was wrong with them?"

"They didn't fit," I answered. His voice rising, he said to my back, "What do you expect? They're *jeans.*"

Designing and making my own clothes has been a consuming hobby for many years (dating back, more or less, to my encounter with the salesclerk in 1969), so by now I'm spoiled by the luxury of a custom fit. The clothes I make are the clothes I really live in. About half my waking hours, that includes jeans (photo, facing page).

My jeans fit well because I draft my own pattern; I derived the method and the basic shape from a tailor's patternmaking method that I discovered in Jane Rhinehart's *How to Make Men's Clothes* (1975), which is unfortunately out of print. It's an invaluable book for anyone, male or female, who is serious about clothesmaking. A draft is an ingenious and accurate way of communicating a pattern without having to print it full-scale, which allows for variations based on different body measurements. Drafts don't eliminate the need for muslin test garments, because they don't automatically deal with posture problems; they simply provide a carefully length-and-width adjusted version of whatever pattern the draft is for. You'll find my jeans draft on p. 64 and instructions for using it below.

The draft is for men's jeans, so women who can comfortably (or almost) wear men's jeans will also find it useful. If your measurements include a big difference (more than 10 in.) between waist and hips, and you like jeans that are fitted in the waist, perhaps you'll find that my analysis is a good starting place for adapting a women's pants draft. I have a few suggestions for modifying the draft for a female shape. The construction is the same for male or female, but before we get into that, let's see why classic jeans look the way they do.

The jeans shape: Secrets revealed

Five pockets and indigo denim do not a pair of Levi's make. A tight fit is even less important; it took me years of tinkering with Rhinehart's pattern for classic slacks to understand that jeans aren't merely undersized slacks. No, the trick to making an authentic pair of jeans lies in the shape;

Jerry Sider's jeans, facing page, don't give away their secret too easily; the extra something is that they're custom-fitted and handmade.

and that shape depends on the design of the crotch, and, to a lesser extent, the leg.

Look at the angle of the fly seam in the top drawing on the facing page. It's angled farther away from the vertical than the fly on the slacks. When slacks are zipped, the fabric around the crotch hangs relatively straight. But when jeans are zipped, the angle of the fly seam causes a slight pouch to form at the front of the crotch. The waist dips slightly, and the front of the pants tends to pull horizontally across the hips. The relatively shallow (from front to back) crotch narrows the top of the leg and pulls the waistband down to the top of the hips.

Compare the position and shape of the legs in the two pattern fronts. On the slacks, the leg is more or less centered between the crotch point and the outseam; from the knee to the cuff, the leg is symmetrical. The jeans leg is set farther to the outside, away from the crotch, and the cuff isn't exactly centered under the knee. When a human being puts on the jeans, the wide-set leg is bent inward. A break occurs at the top of the leg, and as a result, those nifty horizontal creases radiate from the crotch.

Here are some suggestions for adapting the pattern for women's jeans. Obviously this pouch business is inappropriate. Making the center-front waistline (point 9 on the draft) only ⅛ to ⅜ in. from point 1 will flatten out the front of the crotch and make the waist fit more comfortably across the top of the lower abdomen.

You might want to make the crotch and top of the legs snugger; simply trim a strip from the top of the back inseam that tapers into the thigh. Or it may be that the extra room in the crotch will allow you to wear the pants higher on your waist than would be comfortable for a man. Pull 'em up, take in the waist a bit, and the jeans will begin to curve and hug in all the right places.

Taking measurements

Determining your measurements is the beginning of the design process. If you or your subject has been wearing jeans that would be perfect if they were just a bit longer in the rise or a touch looser in the waist, this is your opportunity to incorporate those modifications into your pattern.

Measure the hips in the usual way, over the underwear, and parallel to the floor all the way around, rounding off the measurement to the nearest ½ in.

The waist measurement is actually taken around the top of the hips, about 1½ in. below the real waist. Or you can measure the inside of the waistband of a pair of pants that fit comfortably at that height. The best way to obtain the other three measurements is also to measure a pair of jeans that's close to what you want, adding

or subtracting to the measurements to make them perfect. Measure the outseam (top of the waistband to the end of the leg) and the inseam (crotch to the end of the leg), and subtract the second measurement from the first to get the length of the rise.

Drafting: First steps

The basic tools for drafting are simple; heavy paper in rolls (brown wrapping paper is good), sharp pencils, clean erasers, a curved ruler, and a drafting square.

I only recently discovered the drafting square, available in some fabric stores and from most tailors' suppliers. The square will enable you to draw perfect right angles (and we'll be making lots), and it will serve as an ordinary 24-in. ruler, but its main virtue is that it displays measurements that are specifically required for the drafting process. If you scan the instructions in the draft, you'll see things like: "12 to 14 is one-fourth the cuff measurement minus ¼ in." If your cuff is 16½ in., you could divide that by 4 or just look at the square: along one edge you'll see "4ths." Next to that, you'll see numbers, as in the photo below. Find 16½ in the "4ths" section, and that will be one-fourth of 16½ in., measured from the corner of the square. If the number you need is outside the "4ths," the next section is "Halves," so just double any of the numbers there, and you'll be able to read that section in fourths. Along the other arm of the square you can read in "12ths," "6ths," "3rds," and so forth. If you don't feel like investing in a square, you can use a record album. It will give you an acceptable 90° angle, and a ruler and a calculator can supply the odd dimensions, but the numbers will be in decimals.

Unroll a length of brown wrapping paper 1 ft. longer than the length of your out-

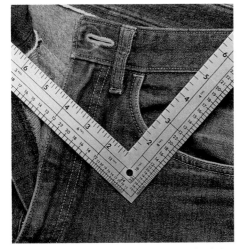

The tailor's square is also a primitive calculator; to divide a measurement into fourths, just find your dimension on the "4ths" scale and measure from the corner of the square.

A jeans draft for men

Front

To start the front draft, draw a straight line—about 1 ft. longer than the pants outseam—down the center of a sheet of paper. Point 1 is on that line, 3 or 4 in. from the top.

• From point 1 to 2 is the outseam measurement minus the waistband width (1½ in. is the standard waistband width).

• 2 to 3 is the inseam measurement.

• 3 to 4, the knee position, is one-half the inseam minus 2 in.

• 3 to 5 is one-twelfth the hip measurement. Draw parallel lines through 1, 2, 3, 4, and 5 perpendicular to line 1-2, extending about 3 in. to the left and about 1 ft. to the right.

• 5 to 6 is one-fourth the hip measurement minus ¼ in.

• 7 is 6 in. directly below 6 (use the square), the same distance from line 1-2 as 6.

• 3 to 8 is one-twelfth the hip measurement minus 1 in.

• 1 to 9 is ¾ in.

• 9 to 10 is one-fourth the waist measurement minus ⅜ in.

• 11 is midway between 5 and 6.

• Draw a vertical line the length of the pattern through point 11, parallel to line 1-2. Point 12 is where the line crosses the horizontal line through point 2.

• 13 is where line 11-12 and the line through 4 intersect.

• Establish the circumference of the cuffs. I use 16 in. Overestimate if in doubt; it's easy to narrow cuffs.

• 12 to 14 is one-fourth the cuff measurement minus ¼ in.

• 12 to 15 is the same distance as 12 to 14.

• 16 to 4 is ⅛ in.

• Connect the dots, and the pattern will appear: Draw a line

from 9 to 5; continue the line in a shallow curve to 8. Starting again at 9, draw a line perpendicular to line 9-5 until it's about ⅜ in. below line 9-10; then curve up to 10. Draw a curve from 10 to 6; the last inch should be vertical.

• Extend the line to 7.

• Connect 7 to 15 with a straight line. Then redraw the angle at 7 as a smooth curve.

• Connect 16 to 14 with a straight line.

• Draw a shallow curve from 8 to 16 that straightens out 2 to 3 in. above the knee line and flows smoothly into line 16-14. The angle at 8 should be slightly larger than 90°.

• 17 is the intersection of line 4-13 and the outseam; label it after you've drawn the pattern outline.

• My pocket line begins 4¾ in. left of 10 on the waist edge and ends 3 in. below 10 on the side seam. The line begins vertically at the waist, curves broadly, and ends horizontally.

• I locate the fly notch by making the distance from point 8 to the notch the same as the distance from point 8 to point 3, measuring on the curve. Transfer all the point numbers to the inside of the pattern outline and cut it out.

Back

The draft for the back has three parts: the leg and crotch, the slope, and the yoke.

• On a second sheet of paper, the same length as the first, draw a line down the center. Lay the pattern front on the paper, 4 or 5 in. from the top, aligning the vertical line 11-12 with the line you've just drawn, and draw around it. Draw extensions of the

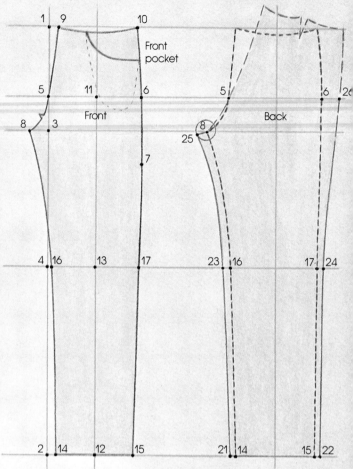

horizontal lines on the pattern-back paper and transfer to the outline points 5, 6, 8, 14, 15, 16, and 17. Points for the back will start with 21; work from the bottom up.

• 14 to 21 and 15 to 22 is ½ in.

• 16 to 23 and 17 to 24 is ½ in.

• 8 to 25 is one-twelfth the hip measurement minus 2 in.

• To locate point 25, draw a circle with point 8 as the center and the distance from 8 to 25 as the radius. Now, measure a straight line from point 8 to point 16 and subtract ¼ in.; measure off

this new length from point 23 to where it touches the circle. That point is 25.

• 26 is 1⅝ in. from 6.

• Connect 21 to 23 with a straight line.

• Connect 22 to 24 with a straight line.

• From 25 draw a curve to 23 so it flows into line 21-23.

Pattern-back guide

The angle and length of the center-back seam in the flat pattern determine how the seat section will fit the seat from side to side and from

seam and tape it to a hard, smooth surface; I use the floor. Draw a line down the middle of the paper, and mark point 1 on the line 3 or 4 in. from the top. The first steps in the draft involve laying out the outseam and inseam measurements and establishing the knee level, along the line and in relation to point 1. We'll draw lines at right angles to the first line at those points, creating a simple grid. All the remaining points

that we need to establish the jeans front will be determined by measurements laid out along these lines; and we'll complete the pattern by connecting the dots, using the curve and the square.

For the back we'll lay out another sheet of paper, we'll trace the front pattern and points onto it for reference, and then we'll start marking off points for the back, up to the crotch level. Above that, we'll have to

draft a separate piece, the pattern back guide, which establishes the slope, or the angle of the seat section (everything that's above the crotch) in relation to the vertical. After aligning the guide with the back draft and tracing around it, the back will be complete, but it will still be necessary to convert the dart section into a yoke, all of which is detailed above. I'll leave the shape and position of the pockets up to you; you

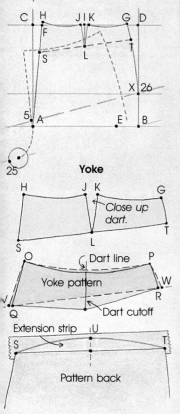
top to bottom in the finished garment. Rhinehart's method establishes that angle and length by incorporating the relevant measurements—waist, hips, and rise—into an extra pattern piece, the pattern-back guide, which, with my modifications, is drawn like this:

• On paper a few inches longer than your rise, draw three 1-ft.-long horizontal lines the same distance apart as lines 9-10 (waist), 5-6 (hips), and 8-3 (rise) on the pattern front. Near the left end of the bottom line, mark point A.

• A to B is one-fourth the hip measurement plus 1½ in.

• Square up from A to find C on the top line; square up from B to find D on the top line. Line C-D equals line A-B.

• A to E is one-fourth the waist plus ⅞ in.

• C to F and G to D are each half of E to B. (In other words, the A to E measurement is centered on the top line.)

• Connect A to F; extend the line ⅛ in. to point H.

• Connect B to G and mark point X where the line intersects the middle horizontal line.

• I is midway between F and G.

• J and K are ¼ in. on either side of I.

• L is 2 in. directly below I.

• Draw lines J-L and K-L.

• Starting at H, draw a line perpendicular to line A-H until it dips ⅛ in. below the horizontal line; then curve up to J. Connect K to G with a curve that dips ⅛ in. below the horizontal line.

• Extend lines A-H and B-G 2 to 3 in. below line A-B.

• Cut out the guide and place it on the pattern back so that point X is touching point 26. Using point X/26 as a pivot, swing the guide up until line A-H touches point 5 (drawing at top left). That establishes the correct slope for the seat.

• Before you trace around the guide, take a few minutes to observe how the back guide works. Move point X on the guide back and forth along line 5-26, readjusting the slope as you go. What you'll see (approximately, since we're not changing the size of the guide) is what happens to the shape of the seat when the hip measurement changes but the waist and rise remain constant. As you decrease the hips (by moving the guide in),

the angle of the slope becomes shallower, and the seat seam shorter; the pants will have a flat vertical curve over the seat. As you widen the hips, the angle becomes steeper, and the seat seam longer, to cover a full seat.

• If you have flat hips but a full seat, try moving point X out ⅛ in. or more from 26 before drawing the slope. For broad hips and a flat seat, move X in before drawing the slope.

• For a snugger seat in all directions, move in X and 26 together; the circumference of the seat will decrease as the slope becomes shallower. Keep in mind that moving the guide only ⅛ in. results in almost a ½-in. change in the length of the seat seam; be accurate in your drawing and conservative in your alterations.

• Draw around the guide from point 5 to point X; then label points H and G on the guide outline. Starting at G, draw a flat curve through point 26; it straightens out about 3 or 4 in. above point 24 and then flows into line 22-24. Draw the outseam curve through point 26 even if you've adjusted the slope so X and 26 don't coincide.

• Line H-5 continues in a curve to 25, passing through, or just above, 8. The angle at 25 should be slightly less than 90°. Cut out the pattern back.

Yoke

On jeans, the dart is converted into a yoke. I make a mark on the outseam of the pattern back 1½ in. down from the waist. I draw a line from that point to the tip of the dart, then continue on to the seat seam for a yoke that's about 2¾ in. deep in the back. As

long as the yoke line goes through the tip of the dart (center drawing), you can tilt it any way you want, but the back should be deeper than the side.

• Draw a line through the middle of the dart extending a few inches past the tip, marking the dart location on the pattern below it, and then cut off the top of the pattern back along the yoke line; the top on each side of the dart will fall into two pieces. Match up the sides of the dart and tape the pieces together, closing the dart. Outline this taped piece on a new sheet of paper and label the corners 0, P, Q, and R.

• Connect Q to R with a straight line, extending the line a bit in both directions. Measure the dart length between line Q-R and the tip; let's call it the dart cutoff.

• On the back pattern, label the two ends of the yoke line S and T. Tape a strip of paper to the pattern back that extends 1 in. above S-T.

• Point U to line S-T is equal to the dart cutoff: it's located on the paper strip along the line you drew through the tip of the dart. Connect S to T with a broad curve through U, and cut along the curve.

• To make the bottom edge of the yoke match the length of the curve S-T:

Mark point V, ¹⁄₁₆ in. from Q.

Mark point W, ¹⁄₁₆ in. from R.

Connect 0 to V with a straight line.

Connect P to W with a slight curve.

Smooth 0 to P with a curve that passes just above the top end of the dart. Make sure the angle at 0 remains 90°. Cut along the new outline, and the yoke is complete. *—J.S.*

---

can be creative, or you can just copy a pair of your favorite jeans.

This draft does not include seam allowances, cuff turnups, or a waistband. You'll probably be making flat-felled seams all over the place, so including allowances for these in the drafting instructions would be needlessly complicated. Once you come up with a pattern you like, redraw it with the seam allowances included, or just note the

allowances on the basic pattern and cut them as you come to them.

My instructions should give you a pair of jeans that are snug but not tight. If you want tight-fitting pants, simply underestimate your hip measurement a little bit; the draft will be reduced evenly in all directions. However, just to play it safe the first time you make your jeans, leave an extra ¼ in. of fabric along the hips and an extra

½ in. along the leg at the top of the back inseam. Remember to preshrink the denim before you cut it.

Construction

The first thing that I do is to sew the yokes to the backs. The flat-felled fold points down: Cut a ⅝-in. seam allowance for the yoke, ¼ in. for the back piece; sew at the seamline, wrong sides together; and then fold

Making a button fly

If you want authenticity, you may as well go all the way; you'll never have the complete low-down, hip-rolling, blue-jeans look without a button fly.

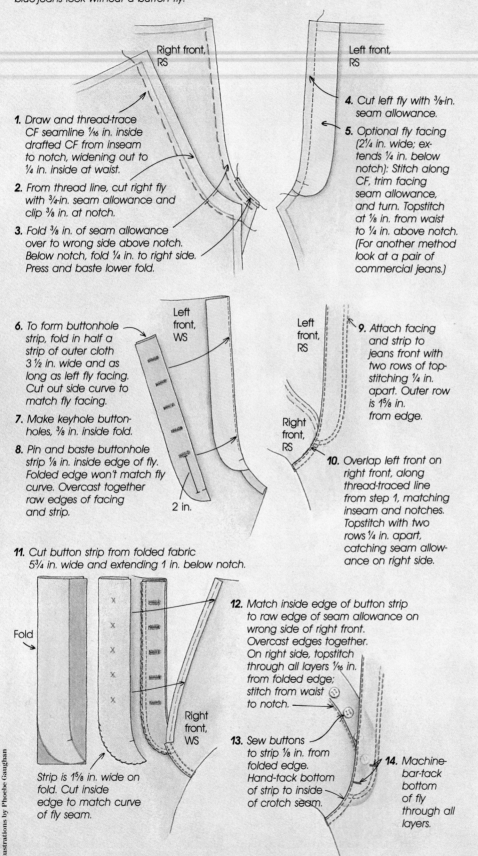

Right front, RS

Left front, RS

1. Draw and thread-trace CF seamline 1/16 in. inside drafted CF from inseam to notch, widening out to 1/4 in. inside at waist.

2. From thread line, cut right fly with 3/4-in. seam allowance and clip 3/8 in. at notch.

3. Fold 3/8 in. of seam allowance over to wrong side above notch. Below notch, fold 1/4 in. to right side. Press and baste lower fold.

4. Cut left fly with 3/8-in. seam allowance.

5. Optional fly facing (2 1/4 in. wide; extends 1/4 in. below notch): Stitch along CF, trim facing seam allowance, and turn. Topstitch at 1/8 in. from waist to 1/4 in. above notch. (For another method look at a pair of commercial jeans.)

Left front, WS

6. To form buttonhole strip, fold in half a strip of outer cloth 3 1/2 in. wide and as long as left fly facing. Cut out side curve to match fly facing.

7. Make keyhole buttonholes, 3/8 in. inside fold.

8. Pin and baste buttonhole strip 1/8 in. inside edge of fly. Folded edge won't match fly curve. Overcast together raw edges of facing and strip.

2 in.

Left front, RS

Right front, RS

9. Attach facing and strip to jeans front with two rows of topstitching 1/4 in. apart. Outer row is 1 5/8 in. from edge.

10. Overlap left front on right front, along thread-traced line from step 1, matching inseam and notches. Topstitch with two rows 1/4 in. apart, catching seam allowance on right side.

11. Cut button strip from folded fabric 5 3/4 in. wide and extending 1 in. below notch.

Fold

Strip is 1 5/8 in. wide on fold. Cut inside edge to match curve of fly seam.

Right front, WS

12. Match inside edge of button strip to raw edge of seam allowance on wrong side of right front. Overcast edges together. On right side, topstitch through all layers 1/16 in. from folded edge; stitch from waist to notch.

13. Sew buttons to strip 1/8 in. from folded edge. Hand-tack bottom of strip to inside of crotch seam.

14. Machine-bar-tack bottom of fly through all layers.

Illustrations by Phoebe Gaughan

the wider allowance over the narrower one and topstitch.

Next are the pockets, front and back. For the back patches, make a cardboard template of the finished shape so both pockets will be the same, and press the seam allowances over it. Stitch down the opening edge; then topstitch the whole thing in place. The only trick to the standard front-scoop pockets is to cut the actual pocketing so that it is out of the way of the side seams, as shown in the draft for the jeans front. I don't French-seam the pocket bags, but simply overcast them. Don't forget the little patch pocket inset on the pocket facing on the right-hand side.

The fly is next; see "Making a button fly" at left for instructions.

Attach the back pieces to the front with flat-felled seams (5/8 in. for the front seam allowance, 1/4 in. in back). Levi's are flat-felled on the inseams, but I'd rather see the decorations, so I just fell the outseams. At the point where the pocket seam joins the back piece, cut away as many underlayers of the flat-felled seam as you can in order to reduce the bulk; make sure that no cut edges are visible in the finished seam. Tack this section firmly in place before you topstitch.

Attach the two back pieces along the seat with a flat-felled seam; the right side should overlap the left. At the point where the yoke seams come together, reduce bulk as described above.

Turn the pants inside out and line up the front and back inseams. If you've used my fly instructions, keep in mind that the true crotch line on the front, below the fly, is the folded edge of the flat-felled seam; it should line up with the true crotch line on back; i.e., the line of topstitching farthest from the flat-felled fold. In one grand gesture, stitch up one leg, across the crotch, and down the other leg.

The waistband is just a big rectangle, folded in half, and as long as the waist seam, plus the width of the right fly and two 5/8-in. seam allowances. The finished width is 1 1/2 in; I add two seam allowances and cut one long edge on a selvage, which self-finishes the band on the inside. Each finished belt loop is 1/2 in. wide and 2 3/8 in. long; you'll need seven loops: two in the front, two at each side, one at the center back, and two in between. You can see the topstitching details in the close-up photo on p. 63. □

If you decide to experiment with Jerry Sider's draft to make a pair of women's jeans, please write to us to tell us about your experiences. —The Editors

Jerry Sider is a writer and producer of audio-visual material in Los Angeles, CA.

Sewing Workout

Fabrics and techniques for constructing stretchy activewear

by Ellen Gienger

xercise is one of the most popular activities today. Runners, walkers, bodybuilders, gymnasts, and dancers have moved beyond wearing old smelly sweats, and their demand for suitable activewear is a new focus for designers. Close-fitting exercise clothes made with stretchy spandex fabrics are comfortable; they're great even for casual evening wear. As an aerobics instructor, I see lots of people who spend hours getting into shape dressed in style.

I design and draft patterns for the clothes I make and sell, but if you want to try sewing some for yourself, commercial patterns are available. Along with information about fabrics and designs, I'll share sewing techniques I use to make garments professional-looking and long-lasting.

A wild array of fabrics

Activewear fabrics, also called swimwear fabrics, come in both cotton/spandex and nylon/spandex blends. Spandex is wonderful because it holds you up and in, so your body looks and feels smaller. (The name Lycra is the registered trademark for span-

Combine spandex fabric and stretchy seams for a garment that moves. The woman in the foreground wears a jumper over an excellent basic garment, a black unitard. The woman in the background wears a cotton dance skirt over a jumper to really absorb sweat. (Photo by Dale Mincey)

dex products of the Du Pont company.) Stretch varies; the rule of thumb is the more spandex a fabric contains, the greater its stretch. Fabrics generally have 10% to 20% spandex and 80% to 90% nylon or cotton. Two-way stretch fabrics, called *raschels*, have 50% stretch in one direction and 25% stretch in the opposite direction. Four-way stretch fabrics, called *tricots*, stretch 100% in all directions.

Stretch is important when laying out a garment. When using raschels, always make sure the direction with the most stretch goes around the body. Most nylon/spandex prints are raschels, so be careful if you use them for garments like tights or unitards (photo at left) that need a lot of stretch in one direction. Raschels are generally used for leotards, jumpers, and dance pants. Garments can be laid out in either direction on a tricot.

Many people prefer stretch nylon because it holds the body like a girdle, yet has more stretch than cotton. If you don't need the extra support, I recommend wearing cotton next to your skin because it absorbs moisture. I can wear a cotton unitard all day, and it makes great ski underwear. Aesthetically, the matte surface of cotton makes a nice contrast when pieced with glossy nylon in the same garment. A benefit of layering a cotton garment and a nylon one is that the layers shift very little on the body when the wearer moves.

Stretch fabrics (photo at right) are available in solid colors, prints, and a variety of textures and specialty surfaces. Specialty fabrics include shiny and thick *stretch satin*; *fancy surface*, a flat fabric with a textured design knitted in; *glistening sheer* stretch nylon; *stretch lace*; and *ribbed* solids in both nylon and cotton. Prices range from $2.50 to $18 per yard.

I look for prints and colors that match current fashion trends. Neon colors are popular this year. Black-and-white prints never seem to go out of style. You can choose solid colors to complement prints. I love metallics, anything with shiny gold, silver, and copper, and animal prints, such as snakeskin, zebra, leopard, and tiger.

Stretch nylon fabrics tend to be the brightest, but cotton colors have been getting more exciting. You can even design your own fabric by painting stretch cotton with Eurotex paint, which is available from Cerulean Blue Ltd., Dept. T, Box 21668, Seattle, WA 98111-3168; (206) 443-7744. Eurotex colors are strong and can be washed. Prewash the fabric so the paint will fuse well.

When you buy fabric, make sure you check it for defects. Assume you are buying seconds unless the dealer specifies otherwise. The sources on page 70 will all mail order fabrics.

Stretch fabrics come in fashionable colors with varying surfaces. If cotton/spandex or nylon/spandex (across top) don't come in colors you need, paint your own (far right). Newest fabrics include (horizontally from center to bottom) tricot lace, dotted metallic, Glistenette, and crinkled matelassé.

Styles and design

A wonderful characteristic of activewear is that one garment can fit a range of sizes. I draft most patterns to fit an average person, size 6 to 12. For a smaller or larger size, I decrease or increase the measurements by only ½ in., and the most I've ever added for a large size is 1 in. Most activewear designs—unitards, pants, jumpers, skirts, and tubes—require less than two yards of fabric. I make a few basic shapes that can be worn separately or together.

A unitard is a combination of tights and leotard in one garment. I make mine with only two seams—one along the inner legs and one down the back—which works especially well with prints, since there are no side seams to break the pattern. This bodysuit can have various necklines: deep or regular scoop, boat, square, or V. The backs can be T- or O-shaped or scooped.

A jumper is meant to be worn over a unitard or tights. One with a ½-in.-wide thong bottom or with high-cut leg openings, called a French cut, elongates the legs. A larger person need not be intimidated by the thong, since it won't make your bottom look any larger than a regular leotard or sweats would. The thong bottom frees you from having to constantly adjust the leg openings while dancing. If the thong is made at least 2 in. wide, it won't pull tightly between the buttocks. Jumpers can have the same neck and back variations as unitards. It looks great to mix backs; for exam-

ple, you can wear a scoop-back unitard with a T-back jumper.

Layering the jumper over the unitard is functional as well as flattering. Two garments give more support in the bust and abdomen than one layer would. I cut the jumpers narrower than most other patterns for greater bust support.

Stretchy tubes may also be worn over the bust for support. Short tubes are useful as belts and tops, while the longer tubes can be worn as skirts or full-length dresses. The tubes—rectangles of fabric with one seam—are 24 in. around and from 8 in. to 30 in. long.

Recently, I designed a dance skirt that is comfortable to wear for aerobic dance or as casual wear. It is made from a tube and a 28- to 32-in.-dia. donut of fabric with a 12½-in.-dia. hole. One tube end is inserted into the hole and stitched in place. The skirt is good for covering heavy thighs.

The color in these basic garments can be combined or pieced to highlight or camouflage different parts of the body. Wear darker colors or subdued prints to disguise flaws and bright colors or bold prints to show off the good parts. Large people should stay away from pastels and white.

Certain prints look flattering on large as well as small figures. Large prints with contrasting colors fragment the body, so your eye moves around instead of focusing on one large shape. You can also achieve this effect by piecing solid fabrics. A recent design of mine with seven pieces, shown in the drawing on page 70, is a good example of this concept.

Patterns to stitches

If I have a pattern idea, I record it with a quick sketch. The sketch reminds me of the number of pieces to cut, the width of the straps or thong, and the color scheme. Next I draw the pattern to scale with a tracing wheel on freezer paper or butcher paper. I use a commercial pattern or a pattern I've already made for the basic dimensions. If a fabric is very stretchy, it will fit a larger person, so I'll decrease the dimensions.

Once I have a draft for a popular style, I make a full, rather than a half, felt pattern for layout. Felt patterns stick easily to stretch fabrics, and they hold up well to repeated use. You won't need pins, so the fabric will lie flatter, which makes it easier to cut accurately.

Working with stretch fabric is difficult at times, and it requires a lot of patience. The heavy, slippery fabric flips and flops and wants to slide off the table. If you are going to work with it on a regular basis, I suggest you have a good-size cutting table. Work with the fabric rather than against it. I use smooth rocks to anchor the fabric in position on the table. Freezer-paper patterns can be tacked to the fabric by ironing them *lightly* using low heat. Wrinkles in the fabric can be ironed out with a dry iron on a low to medium setting. The fabric must be as flat as possible because every bit of extra fabric creates a lot of ease.

Make sure your scissors are sharp. I recommend Gingher's largest shears, which I use to cut one garment at a time. Mark the center and each side of the crotch seam, the curve centers, and the center side seams with small, 1/8-in.-deep snips, rather than tailor tacks, in the 1/4-in. seam

allowances; that way, you will have guidelines when sewing. This is especially important when you are sewing stripes because the fabric tends to stretch during sewing, and you wind up with unequal sides when you get to the end of a seam. Clips also make it easier to stitch around curves.

Be aware of color and placement of prints when cutting out printed fabrics. You may find you'd like to show off special prints to their fullest by widening straps and thongs, cutting necklines higher, or creating cutouts to eliminate certain colors or shapes. The cutting step can sometimes be the dawn of a new design concept. I don't pass up a single idea.

Once the cutting is done, I serge all the seams, leaving the openings that will need elastic—neck, armholes, legs, O-back—for later. For serging, I use a heavy polyester serger thread (American Thread, texture 40, TKT 50), which I buy on 6,000-yd. cones, along with a size 90 ballpoint needle. Many local fabric stores carry serger threads, but not in a large variety of colors or the heavy weight needed for dancewear. I hate making repairs, so I use a heavy-duty thread.

My Bernina serger can accommodate four threads, although I use only three threads for narrower, stretchier seams. Looper tensions and stitch widths vary from machine to machine. My looper tension is generally on 5, but I sometimes change this for different fabrics. (For more information, refer to "Sewing for Stretch," *Threads*, No. 23, pp. 62-65. Details on looper tensions and stitch widths are included.) When I serge elastic, I set my stitch length longer for less bulk, and I shorten it when I sew the seams. I try to match colors exactly, except for unusual colors (such as neon pink and chartreuse) for which I'll use tan, black, or white.

Next I serge swimwear elastic to the wrong side of the opening edges. Swimwear elastic keeps its stretch through repeated washing and exposure to chlorinated water. My favorite is Stretchrite Elastic for Knits, 1/4 in. wide for necklines and armholes, and 1/2 in. to 3/4 in. for waistlines. I buy mine through Payless Drugstores and get a 10% discount; Hancock Fabrics, G Street Fabrics, Nancy's Notions, and Clotilde also carry it.

I feed the elastic through a slot on the regular serger foot that is officially set up for bindings, as I'm doing in the photo at top left. This works beautifully, and keeps the elastic away from the cutter. Apply a little resistance to the elastic so that it shirrs the fabric slightly, as shown in the photos of samples at bottom left. You don't want the elastic to be uncomfortably tight, yet loose elastic causes a "lettucing" effect. It's a delicate balance and takes lots of

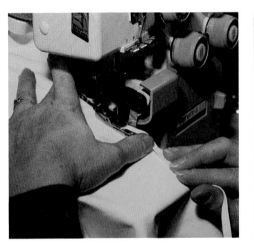
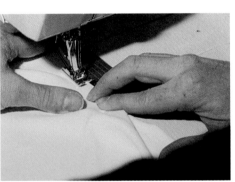

Ellen Gienger serges 1/4-in. swimwear elastic (left) through the slot of the regular foot. Double-needle topstitching (above) gives the garment a finished look. (Photos by Stephanie Hakanson)

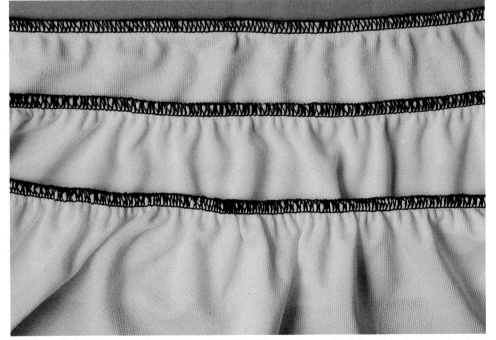

Adjust elastic tension according to the application. Gienger's samples (above) include tension that is too tight (bottom), just right for thong bottoms (center), and more relaxed for necklines (top).

practice to achieve the desired effect; I suggest practicing on some scrap fabric before you stitch the real garment. It is difficult to move around curves and corners while serging the elastic. Move the fabric around the foot with your fingers, keeping the fabric as flat and undistorted as possible, as if you were sewing in a straight line.

While serging the elastic on thongs, pull the elastic tighter on the edges so that they won't stretch out of shape. This works well even for regular leg openings.

Once you have serged the elastic, move to the sewing machine for topstitching. I use regular-weight (50/3) polyester sewing machine thread for topstitching with a 2.0 mm, size 80 double needle, as shown in the photo on p. 69, top right. (I love my Bernina so much I've even named my dog after it. When you sew as much as I do, you need a good sense of humor.) I prefer Metrosene thread, which I think is the best thread available, or Coats & Clark's cotton-covered polyester. I've tried topstitching with serger thread, but it balls frequently and I have to stop regularly to rethread. Needle lube helps to prevent balling.

It is very important that you use a double needle for topstitching. A single line of stitching will not hold up for activewear, and I guarantee you will be repairing the clothes. The back of double stitching is a zigzag, which stretches with the fabric. I set my stitch length at about 4 mm, a fairly long stitch, because I like the look. Be careful not to set it too long or it will pucker when the fabric is relaxed. As you topstitch, pull the fabric slightly to add stretchability and to keep the fabric flat. Be careful not to slide off the edge of the elastic or the stitching will be bumpy and crooked.

Remember, you are sewing for people who work hard and need a garment with lots of stretch. As a test, stretch a sample hard. If the threads pull, the seams will pop while the wearer is exercising. It takes lots of practice to get a great-looking topstitch.

If I am sewing a special, custom-pieced garment, I take the time to change thread colors while topstitching whenever the fabric color changes. It gives an elegant touch to a beautiful garment. I also topstitch in metallic threads if there is a metallic in the fabric. I generally reinforce the crotch, a high stress point, with additional double-needle stitching, about 1½ in. (3 in. total) on each side of the center. Reinforce 2 in. up the back seam from the crotch before stitching the leg seams. □

Ellen Gienger, who designs and makes activewear under her own label, Dance-threads, is an aerobics instructor in Chiloquin, OR.

Patterns

KWIK ● SEW Pattern Co., Inc.
Consumer Department
3000 Washington Ave. N.
Minneapolis, MN 55411-1699
(800) 328-3953
Their home catalog is $2.50 plus $1 P&H; it comes out twice a year. Patterns are the listed price plus 50¢ each P&H.

Stretch & Sew Patterns
Box 185
Eugene, OR 97440
Refer to local Yellow Pages for nearest retail supplier, or write to above address for mail-order information.

Fabrics and notions

DK Sports
Division of Daisy Kingdom
134 N.W. 8th St.
Portland, OR 97209
(800) 288-5223 (orders only)
(503) 222-9033 (information; ask for sportswear department)
Carries nylon/spandex and cotton/spandex fabrics; samples are $1 per group (nylon solids, nylon prints, cotton/poly, heavy nylons). Stocks Prime Moves and Stretch & Sew patterns, swimwear elastic, and double needles. Catalog of kits is $2.

G Street Fabrics
Mail-Order Service
12240 Wilkins Ave.
Rockville, MD 20852
(800) 333-9191 (orders only)
(301) 231-8960 (information)
This gigantic store carries cotton and nylon stretch fabrics, KWIK ● SEW and Stretch & Sew patterns, swimwear elastic, and polyester thread to match almost any color. Samples are $5 for 10; discuss the types you want to see by calling the information number.

Kieffer's Lingerie Fabrics
1625 Hennepin Ave.
Minneapolis, MN 55403
Carries nylon and cotton stretch fabrics, swimwear elastic, and KWIK ● SEW patterns. Catalog with photos of prints and descriptions of solid colors is bulk mailed twice a year; request next catalog by mail. Mail order only, no phone orders.

Looking Good Fabrics
Box 56394
Renton, WA 98058
(206) 271-3336
LGF's entire business, much of it by phone and mail orders, is activewear fabrics. It carries first-quality solids and prints, KWIK ● SEW patterns, and swimwear elastic. Samples: $2.50 for nylons; $2 for cottons; $4 for all.

Thread Discount Sales
5960 E. Florence St.
Box 2277
Bell Gardens, CA 90201
(213) 560-8177, 562-3438
6,000-yd. cones of serger thread. For a free catalog, send SASE.

Commercial patterns

by Amy T. Yanagi

Workout clothes may seem expensive—up to $40 for one leotard—but after I sewed a set, the prices seemed quite reasonable. Making my first sports bra, trunks, and unitard using a commercial pattern took me a lot longer than those little pieces of fabric implied.

Most edges are reinforced with elastic for long wear and shape, which means they each get at least two passes of stitches whose zigs and zags triple the seam length. The other tricky part is the fit: It's better, at least in my mind, to have the garment a little snug than too loose. Either way, the stretch stitches are tedious to remove. But there are lots of exciting fabrics to choose from, and once you have a basic outfit that fits, you can add details you won't find in

Color scheme for a person with large bust, small waist, average hips.

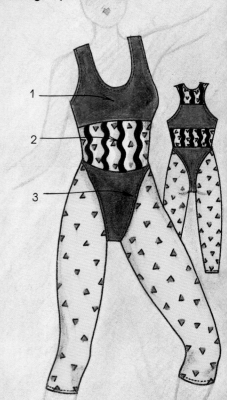

Minimize bust (1) with a dark fabric. Highlight waist (2) with a bright color or print. Highlight or downplay hips (3) by using a light or dark color. Select unitard or tights fabric based on what you wear over it. Continue the same color scheme for the back, as shown.

stores. Here's what I discovered.

Both Stretch & Sew and KWIK • SEW specialize in multisize patterns for garments made with knit and stretch fabrics and provide styles for all sorts of exercise from ice-skating to biking. Both have recently issued patterns for unitards, bike pants, and trunks. KWIK • SEW offers pattern #1567, which includes a sports bra, tights, and trunks; #1935 and #1862, a unitard without and with a front center seam respectively, together with thong-bottom trunks; and #1680, #1288, and #1326 for leotards. Stretch & Sew offers pattern #308 with unitard, leotard, bike pants, sports bra, and pants all in one; #304 with bike pants, skating dress, and leotard; and #312 for tights and bike shorts.

The patterns clearly state the *minimum* amount of fabric stretch required and the garment's final dimensions. With this information and a little testing, you can make a garment that suits your sense of a comfortable squeeze. I'll use the dimensions and instructions from a KWIK • SEW pattern for a unitard to explain.

Start by checking the amount of stretch in your fabric and how you want it to fit. Cut a strip of fabric at least 2 in. wide (or just use the fabric uncut), parallel to the stretchiest direction, and make it long enough to wrap around the widest part of your body that the garment will cover. If you're making a pair of trunks, for example, cut the strip long enough to just wrap around your hips without tension. Mark the fabric strip in 1 in. increments, then stretch it around your hips and pin it when it feels the way you like. Measure how much fabric it takes, and compare it to the pattern's final dimensions. The pattern I used suggests that someone with 38-in. hips should cut fabric following the guidelines for a size medium. The finished garment's hip dimension, which is printed in a chart on the pattern, is 34¼ in. (the fabric must stretch only 3 to 4 in.). But suppose you like the feel of a 30-in. fabric strip (the fabric must stretch 8 in.), which is closer to the final dimensions for size extra small, or 31 in. You'd use the guidelines for the extra small in the hip area. Be sure to check the ease in each piece, because it varies according to the garment's function. When I made a sports bra using the dimensions from the pattern envelope (without testing the fabric stretch and fit as suggested above), I felt like I was being hugged by a boa constrictor; yet the unitard and trunks I made following the same guidelines could have been tighter.

The pattern and envelope indicate the back neck-to-waist, crotch, and inseam crotch-to-floor measurements that each size will fit. Lengthen or shorten the pattern using these numbers and your own measurement; you can't make adjustments by measuring the pattern. The unitard, for example, is meant to fit a person with a 31½-in. inseam as measured from crotch to floor. If your inseam is 27 in., shorten the pattern by at least 4½ in.

Stretch garments can't be mocked up in muslin, and a fitting before any elastic is in place doesn't tell you much either. Elastic defines the edges and pulls the fabric into place; conversely, a garment without elastic will sag deceptively around the neck and armholes and will gap at the waist and legs.

Stitching activewear is an opportunity to try out a three-stitch zigzag and a double needle if your sewing machine is so equipped; with my ten-year-old Bernina Nova, I could have used a zigzag or overlock as well. When the machine is set at maximum stitch width and about a 1 mm stitch length, a 3-st zigzag makes a pattern of ¼-in.-high waves; every rise or fall of a wave has three stitches. It's ideal for attaching elastic because it is stretchy yet less bulky than regular zigzag stitching.

The pattern instructions tell you the amount of elastic to cut for each edge and how to apply the elastic by stitching the ends together, dividing both the elastic and the garment edge into quarters, and matching quarter marks for pinning and stitching. However, if you modify the pattern by adding a scoop neck, O-back, etc., you'll need to measure the pattern to determine the elastic length. The elastic lies flat if it is cut the same size or just slightly larger than the circumference of the opening (plus enough for overlap). If the elastic is cut too small, it creates puckers when the edge is turned under for topstitching. After pinning the circle of elastic at quarter marks, I used the presser foot as a third hand to anchor both layers while I stretched the elastic, flattened the fabric, and pinned it at eighths. Be careful not to stretch the fabric beyond its original shape.

The double needle is threaded from two separate spools but still requires only one bobbin. A universal-point double needle in a size 12 is good for stitching through the layers of fabric and elastic without skipping stitches. The needles come in widths from 1.7 mm to 4.0 mm and in several weights. Schmetz also makes size 11 stretch double needles in two widths, 2.5 mm and 4.0 mm.

Amy T. Yanagi is managing editor of Threads.

Unitard

Thong trunk

Leotard

Sports bra

Bike pants

Embroidery with Texture

A surprising blend of color and depth comes from one simple stitch

by Karina Martens

texture and color have motivated me for as long as I can remember. As a child, I would stand in front of the beautiful colors of embroidery floss in the sewing store, imagining which ones I would take if I could. Finally, my mother agreed to buy me the colors I wanted if I promised to learn embroidery. I began with a transfer pattern but quickly found that it was much more fun to create my own designs. I now use satin stitch almost exclusively. I think this stitch appeals so strongly to me because of the many ways you can arrange the parallel groups of thread and blend colors to produce different textures.

Texture

The type of fabric you choose to embroider is not critical: I've been embroidering skirts all over, making them into an entirely new fabric, as shown on the facing page and at right. Since my embroidery completely covers the fabric, adding weight and thickness, I use a variation of satin stitch that does not cover the back side of the fabric (see *Threads*, No. 46, p. 16, for a drawing of surface satin stitch). This also saves a lot of floss. While working on my first skirt, I discovered that if the stitches are laid down in a triangular pattern, an illusion of three-dimensionality is formed. I'd worked fairly large triangles on the background of the first skirt, and I wanted to know what would happen if I sewed in smaller triangles and how varying thicknesses of thread would affect texture.

The green borders of the skirt are sewn in tight triangles, while the rich blue section at the top is sewn in larger, less precise triangles. The smaller the triangle, the more dramatic the texture appears. Texture is also enhanced by using the full

six plies of thread because the thickness adds depth. I used three-ply thread on the band of women, however, so I could do more detailed work.

Color

Playing with color is my favorite part of embroidery. Choosing colors is a gradual process. If you know what you want for a specific area, pink and yellow flowers, for instance, embroider the flowers and then take the work to the fabric store, hold it up to the racks of embroidery floss, and see what jumps out at you.

You can blend colors using combined

Author Karina Martens uses allover embroidery to restore her old skirts. The "Women's Skirt," which she wears here, used to be a three-tiered white cotton skirt. Now it celebrates the achievements of women in riotous texture and color.

Photo by David Waugh

thread. For example, you get a rich purple effect by using two skeins of embroidery floss: three strands of deep purple combined with three strands of dark blue. The blue at the top of the skirt shown here combines two strands each of three shades of blue. You can see both colors on the facing page.

The best way to avoid ending up with a jumbled ball of embroidery thread is to pull out ends from all the skeins of thread you want to combine, cutting them together into 18- to 24-in. lengths until all the thread has been pulled out. Then separate and recombine one set of colors at a time, knotting the ends of each combination to keep them together.

Tips for embroidery on garments

Since I work on already-made clothing, the size and shape are predetermined. But thick embroidery changes how a garment hangs, making it much stiffer. A garment's shape partially dictates a pattern design, but there is a lot of room for creativity. You can mark with a permanent ink ballpoint pen, since all the lines will eventually be covered.

Embroidering over gathers creates a deeply buckled fabric. Basting gathers flat beforehand helps, as does embroidering across them rather than following them lengthwise. It's also a good idea to work solid areas of color over gathers.

Another challenge presented by embroidering on already-made clothing is the fastenings. I remove buttons and snaps, embroider over where they go, and then replace them. Zippers can be outlined with trim or covered with a ribbon or embroidered placket. □

Karina Martens has recently graduated from the University of Wisconsin at Madison and currently lives in Colorado.

Two Jackets in One

Reversibility starts with pairing the right fabrics and selecting a simple pattern

by Alice Berry

What does it take to make a reversible garment? To begin with, think of it as two sided, rather than as an outer jacket and a lining. I've been making garments based on this idea for years now and have developed a construction sequence that will give you reliable results. It's not much extra effort; in fact, it's simpler than making a jacket with facings and a lining. The reward comes in getting two garments, and with pants and a skirt, you'll have four different outfits. You can cover the territory from business to dress to casual just by playing with your clothes. And, as you'll see further on, it can open up a lot of possibilities for collar insertion and design.

I have three rules when I'm designing for reversibility. First, keep the shape simple; the more complicated the cut, the more likely the jacket is to fight back as you make it. Second, make sure the fabrics are physically compatible; nothing will give you more grief than forcing together fabric types that don't get along. Third, make every effort to pick colors and textures for the opposite sides that go with each other and that will each look good on the same person. I'll discuss these ideas in more detail, then go step by step through the process I use to make virtually all of my reversible garments.

Choosing patterns

The classic pattern with sleeve set into an armhole above a side seam is the least likely to reverse well; easing all four sleeves so that they look good turned in both directions can be done, but it's not easy. I've had good results over the years with raglan, dolman, and kimono sleeve

patterns (see *Threads*, No. 43, p. 26), as well as with boxy blazers and basic shirts that can be constructed flat. I've also been inspired by certain Japanese, French, and Italian designers to come up with cuts of jacket that are more interesting to me structurally, like the ones in the photos in this article; a few workable pattern shapes are in the drawing on p. 80.

With any shape of garment it's best to eliminate as many seams as possible—there's less to go wrong that way. Since I design all my own patterns, I start out with only what I need, but if you're working with a commercial pattern, choose one without a lot of seams, and see if you can eliminate any that it has, like a straight center-back seam or a side seam. Two-piece sleeves don't work unless all the seams are straight. It's also very important that each piece be cut exactly on grain (more on grain later), and from fabric that is grain-straight. You can cut some pieces on both layers on the crossgrain, as long as the fabrics are stable and similar, and the garment is boxy, not fitted. Otherwise, your garment may never hang right. Bias-cut garments are possible and a lot of fun, but they can be risky, especially if the two fabrics are very different.

Shoulder pads don't work in reversible garments. Even if they aren't initially shaped to fit the curve of the shoulders, they'll take on a shape after hanging or wearing for a while, and won't easily reshape when reversed. A padded or quilted yoke is a possible exception, but the best way to get shoulder emphasis is to wear the pads on a garment underneath, allowing space for them in the cut of the unpadded shoulders.

There are a variety of ways to approach

pockets in a reversible garment, the simplest of which is a patch pocket, perhaps on one side only. You can also insert pockets in a side seam. Stitch the single pocket layer to the garment to form the pocket. Normal welt pockets also work, if they're not too bulky.

Pairing fabrics

Fabric is the key to the success of any garment, and that is doubly true with a reversible piece. Each fabric has to work well with the shape of the garment as well as with its opposite-side fabric. The most failsafe combination is two colors of the same fabric, because both will drape in the same way, but the fun comes in putting two very different fabrics together. In the photo on p. 80 are three combinations that I've selected for future garments.

Fabric structure—The two fabrics you choose should be similar in weight so one is not overpowering. Lightweight fabrics are usually the best choice. Also consider fiber content and shrinkage. Prewashing is always a good idea for washable fabrics. Generally, two fabrics of the same fiber and the same type of weave or structure will work together, but similarity of structure is more important.

Whatever fabric you choose, the more stable, the better. By "stable" I mean the resistance of the yarns to movement and shifting within the weave or knit. The worst symptom of instability is when a fabric drapes inconsistently. Rayon fibers and crepe yarns are the worst offenders. That doesn't mean you can't use them—simply be cautious. Be wary of any very slinky fabric or very loose, stretchy knits. Wool crepe is usually more stable than

From *Threads* magazine (November 1992) 43:66-71

Why not get two jackets for about the same effort you put into making one? Designer Alice Berry specializes in garments that are completely reversible, like the one modeled here in purple linen backed with a multihued silk. Reversible jackets are actually easier to make than lined, non-reversing ones.(Photo by Yvonne Taylor)

Fabric combinations can make or break your reversible project. Here are Berry's choices for her next three combos (clockwise from top): jacquard and dupioni silks in the same color; soft, lightweight linen and a substantial rayon satin (challenging, but it'll be worth it!); and medium-weight linen and cotton twill.

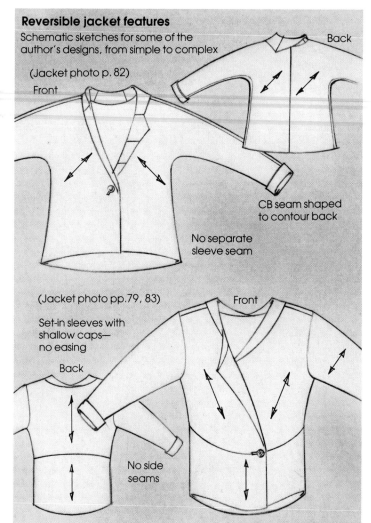

Reversible jacket features
Schematic sketches for some of the author's designs, from simple to complex

(Jacket photo p. 82)

Front

Back

CB seam shaped to contour back

No separate sleeve seam

(Jacket photo pp.79, 83)

Set-in sleeves with shallow caps— no easing

Back

Front

No side seams

rayon crepe and works best if it's used on both sides of the same garment. Gabardines, particularly lightweight ones, work well, as do stable wool and rayon damasks or jacquards.

For an autumn garment, I consider certain combinations classic, and delightful to wear: wool crepe and silk crepe de chine, lightweight corduroy and cotton flannel, wool or rayon challis and wool flannel. For spring, try silk broadcloth with linen, dupioni suiting or rayons with a pongee in those same fibers, cotton poplin with any kind of textured cotton such as dobby, pique, or jacquard.

You can also use knit or jersey fabrics, but only with themselves. No matter how stable the knit, it will continue to stretch over time, while a woven fabric will eventually settle into a shape and stay put. If you choose knits, it's a good idea to reinforce the stress-bearing seams at the shoulders, neckline, and possibly the center-front edges by including twill tape or a strip of woven selvage in the seam, and always to use a stretch stitch. As with a woven fabric, make sure that the weights of the fabrics are compatible and

that neither of the knits is too loose.

A good way to judge whether two fabrics will work together is to hold up a yard or two together, right off the bolt. If one drapes very softly and the other is stiff or bulky next to it, they're not likely to work together. But in the end the only way to be sure is to make the garment. It's the unexpected combination that's the most fun to make and to wear.

Color and pattern—Think about the use you intend for your garment as you choose colors for it. If you want to wear it to work during the day and then out for the evening, one side can be subdued and businesslike, the other brighter for more casual or dressy situations. Sometimes there is enough contrast between two fabrics of the same color but with very different textures. By far my most popular jackets are those of one color, often a black flannel or crepe with a dull or matte finish on one side, reversing to a black taffeta or brocade on the other.

Another way to get a lot of mileage out of a piece is to make it all black on one side and a bright color on the other. De-

pending on how the collar is designed, it is possible to see only black on one side and only the color on the other.

I've often combined two colors, either two very strong ones, or a bright color with a grayed or dulled version of the same hue. When you're balancing two colors, be sure to examine them under a variety of light sources including sunlight and fluorescent light. I once matched a beige and ivory jacquard with the perfect beige linen, or so I thought. When the fabrics arrived in my studio I discovered the jacquard was tinged with green, while the linen was a warm rose.

You can pair a white or light fabric with a strong color or black, even if the light fabric isn't completely opaque. An underlining, either of the fabric itself or a lining fabric (cut on the same grain), can keep the seams from showing through. Or you can treat the layers as one, sewing each seam with both fabrics together, using a flat-fell, bound, or French seam, as long as the seamlines aren't too complex.

When you mix colors with prints, bear in mind that the combination may change the balance of the print. For example, a print with a lot of red and just a little black will look brighter if it is put with black, less so if it is put with a red.

I love to combine plaids and stripes with prints. Some classic combinations include black and white stripes or checks with a black and white geometric or floral print (wonderful for a summer jacket), and any kind of floral or abstract multicolored print with some black in it, paired with a simple black and color check or stripe. It's fun just to try out combinations until you hit upon an unexpected success.

Collars

It's simplest just to leave a collar off a reversible garment, but I find designing or draping collars one of the most enjoyable parts of the process. I usually don't decide on a collar until both jacket bodies are complete, but when I get to that part of the construction, there's a certain strategy I use for all the collars on my reversible garments. The key to making a reversible collar is to make sure it can turn both ways. You can make it as simple as a rectangle set in evenly, or as complicated as an asymmetrical shaped band with a collar set into it, as long as when the garment turns, the collar turns with it. Collars can either be inserted between jacket layers like a piping (as on all the jackets shown here) or sewn to each body separately. Since they need a lot of flex, I often cut the collars on the bias.

I get a lot of mileage out of the same jacket pattern by using many different collars. Starting from a basic lapel cut, I can put in a collar of many different shapes, leave it collarless, make the collar asymmetrical, cut off one lapel, or make a scarf collar by attaching a scarf to the neckline either at the back of the neck or just at the front tips of the lapel.

I'll often add interest to the jacket by doing some sort of fabric manipulation to the collar piece. Tucks, folds, or smocking give density to fabric and often eliminate the need for interfacing. Piecing, quilting, and turning the grain of the fabric to create alternating tones or stripes are other possibilities that make collars, and basic jacket shapes, more intriguing, as you can see in the lower right-hand photo on p. 82.

Typically, I make each side different, since the collar will be seen against both jacket fabrics. If, for example, one side of the jacket is plain, I'll set in the collar to fall so that its plain side will show when that side of the jacket shows. I might then make the reverse side with a fabric that contrasts with the body on the other side, to emphasize the plain/fancy nature of the two sides. ⇨

Adding a window to a reversible garment

The garment in the left-hand photo below shows a decorative technique that I'm very fond of adding to my reversible garments. I cut openings, or "windows," through both layers, into which I can insert all kinds of things—lace, woven ribbon lattices, turned tubes of fabric knotted together, etc.—that will be equally visible on both sides of the garment. The trick is to stitch the edges of the openings on both sides at once as you catch the inserted material to the garment. I use two methods: Edge stitching on top (which can be done to finished garments), and clean finishing on the inside (which I do before the garment's assembled). Edge-stitched openings can be any shape, but clean-finished ones are much easier if the shape has straight or gently curved sides.

The first step for either method is to decide what will go in the window, and what shape the window will be. For the clean-finished method, it's best to keep the window at least 6 in. away from any seamlines, so the garment can still be turned inside out during construction. In either case, I draw the shape in position on the right side of one jacket face (or on one side of the layers sandwiched together right sides out) with chalk, marking the opening about ½ in. smaller all around than the insert.

Pin the area around the opening to secure the layers together, then cut out the opening through both layers,

leaving a ½-in. seam allowance inside the chalk line, so that the cutout is a full inch smaller all around than the insert. Press back the seam allowances on both sides so that the fold lines are on the chalk mark, as you can see in the right-hand photo below. Make sure the edges on opposite sides are even, and clip in the corners and around curves to allow the edges to fold completely back.

For the edge-stitched version, simply slip the insert between the layers, and pin the edges to the insert, aligning them as you pin so the edge stitching will catch both edges evenly. Stitch, press, and you're done.

For the clean-finished version, mark ½-in. seam allowances on the insert, making sure its edges are trimmed. Since you're not working on the finished garment, you can open up the layers and, working on the inside, grab one pair of pressed-back seam allowances, then slip the matching seam allowance on the insert between them. Pin or baste to hold the allowances together, then stitch on the wrong side using the pressed fold line as a guide and going all the way to the end of the clips at each end. Fold the layers back together over your stitching and press, pulling the fabric gently on each side to give a clean edge. Then work your way around the other edges of the insert in the same way. —A.B.

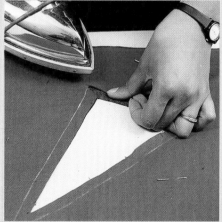

Install a window in your reversible garment and you can insert a decorative detail, like the black lattice at left, that will be visible from both sides. After cutting out the opening shape in both fabrics, with a ½-in. allowance, fold both edges to the inside so the openings are exactly the same.

Reversible collars: *Virtually any shape can be inserted into a neck-line to create a collar, even pieced, asymmetrical shapes like those in the jacket shown at lower right. Berry cut the shapes shown directly below to start draping the split collar she created at left. The longest edge on both pieces went into the seam, but since they could overlap at the center back, the exact length wasn't critical.*

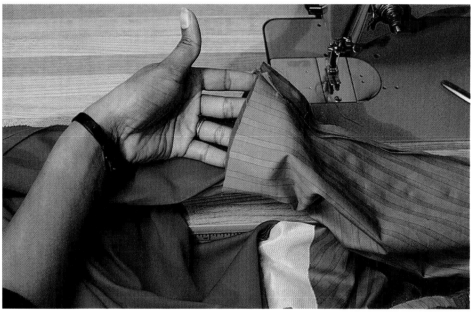

Join the sleeve ends with the two jacket layers facing each other and wrong side out. Fold one sleeve's hem back a few inches and insert it in the opposite sleeve so that right sides are together as shown above. Then sew around the edge to complete the cuff.

For the pink jacket shown in the top two photos above, I chose to make two collars, overlapping them at center back. The shapes I started with are shown in the top right-hand photo. As I draped the shapes on the form, with the completed jacket sides pinned together underneath, I trimmed the collars' outer edges and set them in with opposite sides showing. That way, no matter which side of the jacket was worn facing out, both fabrics would be visible on the collar pieces, as you can see in the top left-hand photo. You could also wear one collar flipped up, so that only one fabric shows.

Construction

There's no mystery to putting together a reversible jacket. Here's the basic outline: I make the two layers and stitch them right sides together along the front edges and neckline, catching the collar in between. Then I stitch along the hem, leaving an opening so I can pull the whole coat right sides out. But first I bring the sleeve hems together and stitch them with the garment still inside out. Let's go over the steps in more detail.

First, I lay out and cut my chosen fabrics as one, with right sides facing each other, and with grain and nap carefully matched. Most jackets will need at least a little interfacing, typically down the front on both sides. Depending on your fabric, you also may want to interface the back of the neckline, and the collar. If your fabric is soft, it's even a good idea to interface the hems at the bottom and sleeves. No matter what fabric I'm using, I almost always interface it with a fusible tricot, since this gives body without adding much weight or thickness. If I'm inserting a decorative window, as described in "Adding a window to a reversible garment" on p. 81, I'll interface the area for that also.

Wool and silk twill team up to form a pair of dressy sides to this slouchy suit. (Photo by Yvonne Taylor)

After I've constructed both the inner and the outer layer and clipped and pressed open all the seams, I match the neckline and any shoulder seams on both layers right sides together and insert the collar, like piping, between them, as if one side were the lining or facing. I pin, baste, and sew the collar to both sides at once, making sure that the underlayer doesn't get pinched into little tucks as I'm sewing around the neckline curve. I usually sew one long seam starting at one hem edge in front, going around the neck, then down the opposite front to the hem. Press the seam and turn right side out.

At this point it's crucial to leave the garment on a form or padded hanger for at least 24 hours so the hems can settle and fall as they wish. Carefully pin or baste all the seams at the shoulder together, but leave the side and sleeve seams free to hang. After the piece has hung, one side will probably have fallen a little more than the other. Since the sleeves have to be the same length, measure them from the neckline, and trim if necessary.

Pin the hems just as they have fallen on the bottom and sleeves, trim the excess fabric, unpin, and turn the jacket inside out. Then sew along the hem, leaving an opening of about 5 in. at some point, along an area with a straight grain if possible. To sew the sleeves together, pull them wrong sides out so they face each other. Turn back both sleeve hems near the hemline on one garment side for a few inches and slip them into the ends of the opposite sleeves so that right sides are together, as in the lower left photo on the facing page. Match the sleeve seams, and sew around the ends.

Turn the jacket right side out through the opening in the hem. I don't like to hand stitch, so to make the opening as small as possible by machine, I reach inside and grab a bit of the hem fabric through this opening and arrange it so that I can continue sewing the hemline closed as far as possible. When I can go no further, I press the hem smooth again and slip-stitch or fuse the opening closed, press the garment, and try it on! □

After living in Paris for four years, clothing designer Alice Berry now lives and works in Chicago. She sells through her own showings and at selected boutiques.

A Surprising Turn of the Pleat

Simple techniques for jacket construction and fabric manipulation

by Lois Ericson

One of the jackets depicted in my article "The Uncommon Closure" (*Threads* No. 22; also shown at left on the facing page) sparked many inquiries from readers interested in making something similar. The pattern I used (Vogue 1930) is no longer available, but I incorporated a lot of techniques into that jacket that could be applied to any pattern.

If it's the pattern that you liked most about the original, it was a simple shape (see the drawings on the facing page), and it wouldn't be difficult to adapt a current pattern for a similar effect. To me, the most interesting thing about that jacket is the manipulated tucks worked on a striped fabric, because I find the resulting color-change effects so attractive. I've made a new jacket (shown at far right on the facing page) that illustrates both the manipulation of the fabric and a few ideas for constructing garments out of it once it's tucked.

Tucking stripes

The idea behind manipulated tucks is very simple: Once stitched, tucks can be folded to either side, so why not fold them in different directions in different parts of the same tucked fabric for a more interesting texture? The tucks can be held in their alternating positions with rows of stitches at an angle to the tucking stitches.

If you tuck striped fabric, the possibilities become much more exciting because of the optical illusions you can create. You can tuck along the stripes so that one color or pattern is all that shows when the tucks are folded one way, and another color or pattern shows when they're pressed the other way.

Choosing stripes—Any repeating stripe can be folded to show a different face on each side of a tuck, but some are easier to work with than others. My favorite striped fabrics, like those in all the garments and examples shown, have only two alternating stripes: usually one plain, "background" stripe, setting off a stronger, multicolored "foreground" one. I tuck these fabrics so that the background color is on one side of the tuck, and the foreground color is on the other.

An easy-to-fold arrangement is when the ratio of the width of the stripes in a two-stripe fabric is about 1 to 2; for example, 1 in. stripes 2 in. apart. An approximately 1-to-1 ratio stripe, like the ones in my jackets, also works well. The drawing on p. 86 shows how stripes in both ratios can be folded for the two-color effect I've described, and shows that 1-to-1 stripes are more efficient because the fabric folds down to two-thirds the dimension of the original, instead of to half as in 1-to-2 fabrics.

Stripes on the lengthwise grain are the most common, but once tucked, cross-grain-striped fabrics are easier to cut garments out of because the tucks reduce the length of the fabric, not the width. In whatever direction the stripes run, you'll need at least two or three times more fabric than if you used it untucked. Both printed and woven stripes work well, but be sure printed stripes are accurately on grain, so the tucks don't ripple.

When I cut out the pattern, I arrange the pieces on the tucked fabric in whatever way looks best for that pattern, without worrying about whether I'm cutting with the grain or on the bias. I've never had any trouble as a result, perhaps because I usually select medium-weight fabrics without a lot of drape. The stitched-down tucks also seem to increase the stability of the fabric.

Creating the tuck—With any fabric, first identify a stripe you want to emphasize. Then fold the fabric on the outside edge of the second occurrence of that stripe, counting in from the edge of the fabric, and align it with the inside edge of the first stripe of the same color (left-hand drawing on p. 86). The resulting fold underneath is where the machine stitching will go. Check the effect by folding the tuck back; does only one other color show? Adjust the position of the fold until it works, then each remaining tuck will be the same. There's no need to iron each tuck; simply fold and finger-press, then stitch the length of fabric you need to tuck.

When the stitching is complete, press the tucks to one side, then, about an iron's width away, press another section of tucks in the opposite direction. This will give you an approximation of the final appearance. After the pattern pieces are placed on the fabric, the exact placement of the folds can be changed before you stitch them down. ⇨

Pattern shapes for Ericson's original jacket

Front

CF insert

Back

Insert continued from front.

Precision folding and tucking of striped fabric created the changing colors and textures on Lois Ericson's original jacket (above) and new jacket (right). (Right-hand photo by Susan Kahn)

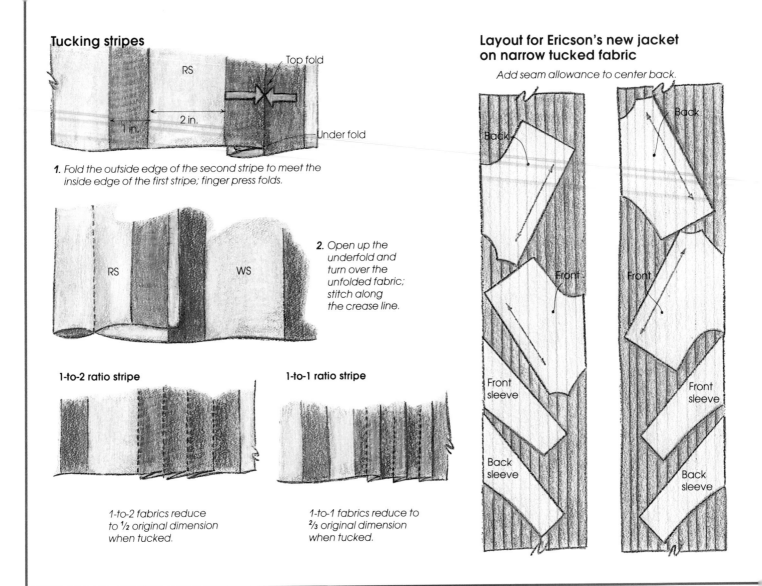

Tucking stripes

RS

2 in.

1 in.

Top fold

Under fold

1. Fold the outside edge of the second stripe to meet the inside edge of the first stripe; finger press folds.

RS   WS

2. Open up the underfold and turn over the unfolded fabric; stitch along the crease line.

1-to-2 ratio stripe

1-to-2 fabrics reduce to ½ original dimension when tucked.

1-to-1 ratio stripe

1-to-1 fabrics reduce to ⅔ original dimension when tucked.

Layout for Ericson's new jacket on narrow tucked fabric

Add seam allowance to center back.

Back

Back

Front

Front

Front sleeve

Front sleeve

Back sleeve

Back sleeve

Selecting patterns

The simpler the pattern, the better, as long as it's interesting. I usually choose one that has an intriguing cut, but not many pattern pieces. For my new jacket, I used Vogue's 7906. Other patterns I liked this year were Butterick 4386; Simplicity 9875; McCall's 4925; and Burda 4921, 4911, and 4958.

I like to find ways to set off the manipulated fabric against sections of the same fabric untucked, as I did on the center front of the original jacket, so I look for patterns that are already pieced in some simple way. Any pattern could, of course, be cut apart and reassembled to create internal seamlines. Sections of the garment could also be covered with untucked fabric, either by appliquéing or by tacking on faced pieces, or even by cutting and binding holes to reveal untucked layers underneath.

In the same way, completely new pattern pieces can be created and attached to the finished coat, or incorporated into the construction. The tucked panel that's

attached to the sleeves on the original jacket wasn't part of the pattern. It's simply a faced strip with bound edges that stretches from wrist to wrist across the jacket back, stitched down only along the forward edge. The fabric was a leftover strip from cutting out the pattern.

Cutting out

When the fabric is made narrower by tucking, it sometimes takes ingenuity to cut out a pattern. Both the original jacket and my newer version have dolman sleeves, which attracted me to the patterns right away. For the new jacket, however, I cut the sleeves off to fit the pattern on my lengthwise-tucked fabric, which had shrunk from 45 to 22 in. wide. I laid the front pattern pieces on the tucked fabric and played with different alignments of the grain until I found a satisfactory placement. At that point I simply marked the front pattern where it extended over the edge of the fabric, checked that the back would fit if the sleeves were cut off at the same place,

and cut the pattern along that line. Because of the covered seam finish I used (described below), it wasn't necessary to add seam allowances to the sleeves; however, I did add them for the standard seam at center back. The right-hand drawing above shows the final layout.

When I actually cut out the individual pieces of a tucked project, I cut them one at a time so that I can carefully consider the position of the tucks. After the pieces are cut, I machine stitch across the tucks to hold them in place. The stitching can be a single inconspicuous row, or more obvious, perhaps made with a double needle or even with a contrasting satin or other decorative stitch. I experiment on tucked scraps.

Before I use up all my scraps in experiments, however, I consider if any of the leftovers could be used on the garment, like the sleeve strips mentioned above, or if they could even become a new garment. That's how the vest in the photo on the facing page evolved; the front is made entirely from the scraps left over

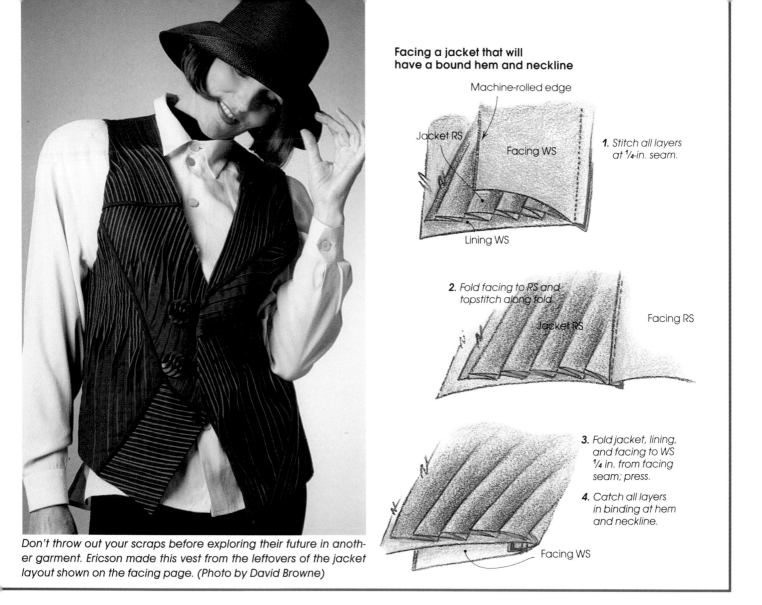

Facing a jacket that will have a bound hem and neckline

Machine-rolled edge

Jacket RS

Facing WS

Lining WS

1. Stitch all layers at ¼-in. seam.

2. Fold facing to RS and topstitch along fold.

Jacket RS

Facing RS

3. Fold jacket, lining, and facing to WS ¼ in. from facing seam; press.

4. Catch all layers in binding at hem and neckline.

Facing WS

Don't throw out your scraps before exploring their future in another garment. Ericson made this vest from the leftovers of the jacket layout shown on the facing page. (Photo by David Browne)

from the jacket on p. 85. I was determined to make them work into a garment after I found those buttons!

Decorative construction

My favorite sewing techniques are quick, decorative, and practical all at the same time. That's why I'm so fond of binding edges, particularly in contrasting fabric, as I've done on both the jackets shown on p. 85. The thin line that binding provides along the edge often adds just the needed touch, plus it's a very quick way to finish the raw edges of both the garment and the lining at the same time. For a ⅜-in.-wide binding like those on both my jackets, I cut bias strips 2½ in. wide, fold them in half, and stitch the two raw edges to the right side garment edge with a ¼-in. seam, catching the lining layer as well. Then I fold the binding to the wrong side and catch the fold by hand to the line of machine stitches.

Before attaching the bindings, I attached the sleeves to the jacket with two 1-in.-wide strips of on-grain contrast fab-

ric, each the length of the entire armscye seam. These strips eliminate the bulky seams of the tucked fabric and also serve as design elements. I stitched one side of each strip to the right side of the jacket side of the seam with ¼-in. seams, and the other side to the sleeve piece; the raw edges butt together underneath the strip, which forms a ½-in.-wide stripe on top of the seam.

The pattern didn't have a lining, so I added one to the new jacket. I simply cut out the pattern (with the sleeves still on) in lining fabric, adding an extra inch at the center-back fold for a pleat.

I caught the lining edges in the binding at the cuffs, hem, and neck. First I finished the front edges with a simple strip of facing cut 4 in. wide and the length of the opening, and stitched as shown in the drawing above. The facings are held in place by the binding at hem and neck.

I'll often repeat the effect of binding with piping and with covered cords in the same fabric, all finished to the same width. On my new jacket, I hand tacked

covered cord (described in my article in *Threads* No. 22) along the center-front openings and around the neck. By leaving short sections of the right-hand cord unstitched wherever there was a button on the left, I created buttonholes at the same time. Where the cord turns the corner at the neckline and hem, I made a simple overhand knot; it looks much better than just bending the cord. To create the piping along the seams at the top of the sleeves, I simply inserted a folded bias strip, without any filler cord, in the seam as I stitched it.

On my original jacket, I faced the shaped bands that curve around the neck, center front, and hem in the ordinary way, just as the pattern described. I let the facing, in contrasting blue, peek out along the front overlap to match the piping, bindings, and cords elsewhere. □

Lois Ericson's latest book, a collection of creative sewing ideas called A Great Put On, *is available from her at PO Box 5222, Salem, OR 97304.*

Topstitching on lapels, epaulets

Wrist strap details

Sewing the Perfect All-Weather Raincoat

Ready-to-wear details add polish and versatility

by Cecelia Podolak

Using a commercial pattern, you can make an all-weather raincoat that rivals the expensive ready-to-wear models. Lots of extra topstitching as shown on the lapels and epaulets in the top inset, and on the wrist straps and loops in the bottom inset; a full permanent lining; plus a zip-out lining/interlining are features that add to the professional finish. The result is a functional garment with comfortable good looks.

the current crop of beautiful raincoats in the stores, many with zip-out insulated linings for extra warmth and versatility, have become the perfect all-weather coats for either rain or snow showers. After admiring some of the finest German ready-to-wear raincoats, some with four-figure price tags, I realized that the styles and essential details were quick and easy enough to duplicate at home for a fraction of the retail price. I knew that most of the sewing could be done on the sewing machine and serger, and rainwear fabrics have become more interesting and accessible to the home sewer. So, I took the plunge and sewed an all-weather coat, shown on the facing page. It's actually a raincoat with two linings, one that's permanent and one that zips out (see "Constructing a warm zip-out lining" on p. 92). I will share what I learned about new fabric technology, notions that work, and ready-to-wear construction techniques.

Fashion rainwear fabrics

The newest versions of polyester and nylon—*microfibers* (short for micro-denier fibers)—are ideal for raincoats. They are comfortable and easy to care for, and have built-in water resistance. A microfiber filament is a fraction of one denier (a unit used to describe filament yarn size). In contrast, most apparel fibers measure from one to seven denier per filament.

Because microfiber yarns have an extremely high number of filaments per strand of yarn, the end fabric is more water- and wind-resistant, two important characteristics for rainwear fabrics. Even though the fabrics have a dense weave, which drops of rain have trouble penetrating, perspiration wicks away from the body through the many air spaces in the yarns, which makes the fabric comfortable to wear. The fabrics are soft and fluid, and many have a brushed or sueded surface. All of this technology increases the cost of microfiber fabrics, so the new fabrics are usually found in better and designer fashions. However, you can purchase the fabric and sew the coat yourself at a great savings. You'll find microfiber rainwear fabrics by such names as Versatech, Tactel, and Vanessa (see the sources on p. 91).

Besides microfibers, look for other high-density fabrics (those having a high thread count), such as nylon or polyester taffeta, crinkle-textured nylon or polyester, or poly/cotton poplin. Again, these fabrics are water- and wind- resistant by nature of their construction. They will not be as comfortable to wear as the microfiber versions, because the filament size is larger. These fabrics are often further treated to help repel water and stains with products like Scotchgard and Zepel, which can be renewed by the dry cleaner or with chemicals you can apply at home. Look for fabric brands such as

Taslan, Supplex, Mountain Cloth, and Nylon Antron Taffeta.

Rainwear fabrics with Gore-Tex and Ultrex are waterproof, windproof, and breathable, due to a microporous membrane or coating. This layer has billions of tiny pores that allow perspiration to escape but are too small for drops of water to enter. These fabrics are more waterproof but less breathable and drapeable than the microfiber fabrics. You'll need to line garments to preserve the backing and seal seams after stitching to maintain the waterproof quality.

Fabrics coated with an outer layer of urethane or rubber are water- and windproof, but less comfortable to wear. Since they do not breathe, perspiration cannot escape through the fabric.

For the coat on p. 88, I used a densely woven, crinkled polyester as the outer fabric and a polyester with a windproof, breathable coating for the permanent lining. For the removable lining section, Thinsulate interlining (see p. 92) adds warmth without bulk, and is layered with a floral polyester lining fabric. In the collar and facings, use a soft, sew-in interfacing or one of the new low-temp. fusibles designed for heat-sensitive fabrics (see *Threads* No. 45, pp. 56-57). Since most rainwear fabrics are washable, make sure that all the coat components are, as well. The fabrics I've mentioned can be purchased at fabric stores, or by mail (see the sources on the facing page).

Most rainwear fabrics have properties that can make sewing and pressing difficult. The synthetics must be pressed at low temperatures, they do not hold a crease well, and they are difficult to ease. Combining just the right pattern with helpful construction and finishing techniques and the proper equipment will ease your way through these difficulties to a beautiful result.

Selecting a pattern

Before you choose a pattern, I recommend that you shop for, try on, and examine better ready-to-wear raincoats to determine the fit and features you want. From my shopping ventures, I developed a wish list that included a permanent lining plus a removable insulated lining, and traditional trench-coat features such as a back vent, epaulets, a tie belt, wrist straps, front and back fabric shields, and comfortable pockets. On the ready-to-wear coats, you'll see that topstitching and edgestitching are applied everywhere, giving crisp edges and a professional finish. I noted the location and width of all this extra stitching, so I could add it to my own coat.

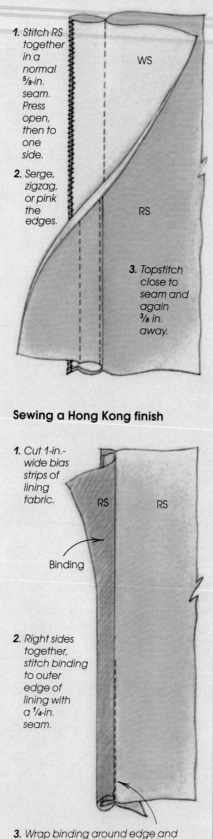

Stitching a mock welt seam

A good choice for fabrics that ravel, a mock welt catches both raw edges in four rows of stitching.

1. Stitch RS together in a normal ⅝-in. seam. Press open, then to one side.

2. Serge, zigzag, or pink the edges.

WS

RS

3. Topstitch close to seam and again ⅜ in. away.

Sewing a Hong Kong finish

1. Cut 1-in.-wide bias strips of lining fabric.

RS   RS

Binding

2. Right sides together, stitch binding to outer edge of lining with a ¼-in. seam.

3. Wrap binding around edge and press. Ditch stitch to secure.

The next step is to take your wish list to a fabric store and study the available patterns for one that comes closest to having the features you want.

In general, choose a coat style with ample ease, rather than a structured, fitted silhouette. You'll want your coat to be comfortable over sweaters and jackets, even with the zip-out lining in place. Patterns with kimono, raglan, or an extended shoulder line with a dropped sleeve are excellent for rainwear. Avoid set-in sleeves and other details which require precise easing, since rainwear fabrics resist easing.

I chose Burda 5773 for its traditional trenchcoat styling that included all the features on my wish list. Burda has discontinued this pattern, but they are hoping to replace it with a new version. Patterns such as Style 1191 and 2189 include many of these features. Other details, such as wrist straps and loops, are easy to add by looking at and measuring ready-to-wear coats, then making simple pattern pieces.

Adapting your pattern

Before cutting the fabric, there are a few adjustments you should make to your pattern to attain a proper fit, to allow for the removable lining, and give a more professional result.

Allowing enough ease—Even though your pattern has a lining, it may not allow enough ease for the extra lining/interlining. Increase the seam allowances to 1 in. for the side seams and shoulders of the outer coat to allow for adjustments after a trial fit. When you're ready to sew, check the fit by basting together the coat and lining/interlining separately, then trying them on one on top of the other. Let out the coat at the seam allowances if you need more ease. Or you can make the zip-out lining slightly smaller (by sewing ⅛-in. larger seam allowances), if the outer coat has the necessary wearing and design ease. Either method allows the lining/interlining to fit smoothly inside the outer coat.

If your coat pattern has adequate ease, I suggest omitting the center-back pleat in both the permanent and zip-out linings, as done in many ready-to-wear coats.

Back-neck facing—If your pattern does not include a back-neck facing, you'll need to add one, since the zipper will be stitched to the facings smoothly around the entire coat. Cut a new pattern piece in the shape of the back neck- and shoulder-line of the coat, and the same width as the shoulder seam of the front facing.

Facing finish—You can finish the coat facings with bias binding, but I have a neat, quicker method which requires an extra ¼-in. allowance. Read about it at right under "Preparing the facings for a zip-out lining." When cutting, add ¼ in. to the inner edge of the facing and interfacing to allow room for the seam.

The necessary notions

If your local fabric store's notions department doesn't stock the following items, mail-order companies carry them (see the sources at right).

Use polyester or cotton-wrapped polyester thread to sew the coat, as both have strength, durability, and elasticity. When serging, I find that texturized nylon thread in the serger loopers results in a softer edge finish.

The Schmetz universal needle 705H in size 10 or 12 sews well on many of the rainwear fabrics. I recommend the Schmetz Jeans needle HJ in size 10 or 12 for microfiber and some of the other high density fabrics. The fine, extra-sharp needle penetrates the fabric and helps to eliminate puckers.

There are several other notions that you may find useful. A Teflon presser foot or a walking foot helps to move the fabric smoothly through the machine. Long quilters' pins with glass heads easily penetrate bulky interlining fabrics. A double-sided basting tape called Wonder Tape holds the zipper in place while you stitch right through it, then dissolves in the first washing or dry cleaning. If you're sewing on coated waterproof fabric, seam sealant will make the seams waterproof after stitching. A drop of Fray Check prevents raveling of the serger thread ends. An opaque Teflon press sheet protects heat-sensitive fabrics during pressing. And a dissolving stabilizer such as Solvy reinforces buttonholes during stitching and helps to prevent puckers.

Coat construction

You'll find that construction goes more quickly if you do all similar processes—such as cutting or sewing or pressing—in batches. Using a rotary cutter, mat, and weights, cut all components of the garment, from fashion fabric to the zip-out lining/interlining. Cutting everything at once helps to ensure that the different sections will fit together. Pin within seam allowances, especially on microfiber and coated fabrics, since pins will leave holes.

Use tracing paper and a wheel to transfer markings, except on microfiber and coated fabrics. For these, use a disappearing pencil or pen, since a tracing wheel may leave permanent holes.

Preparing facings for a zip-out lining—Stitch front and back facings together at shoulder seams. Then stitch the interfacing to the facing right sides together in a ¼-in. seam along the inner edges. This will finish the facing and secure the interfacing, as shown on p. 92. (Add an extra ¼ in. to the inner edge of the facing and interfacing when cutting, if using this method.) After stitching, open the interfacing, and understitch the seam allowance to it (see *Threads*, No. 46, p. 16), which keeps the fabric away from the zipper teeth. Then fuse, if using a fusible.

Making flat, crisp seams—Do as much of the stitching as possible by machine; ready-to-wear uses little if any handsewing, and rainwear fabrics are difficult to

Sources for rainwear fabrics and notions

The Green Pepper
3918 West First Ave.
Eugene, OR 97402
(503) 345-6665
Seam sealer, Thinsulate, Tactel, Taslan, Supplex, Gore-Tex, Ultrex. Catalog $2.

Sundrop Outerwear Textiles
#140 - 1140 Austin Ave.
Coquitlam, BC V3K 3P5 Canada
(604) 936-5236
Tactel, Ultrex, Supplex, windproof Polysilk lining (in author's coat). Catalog $2.

The Rainshed Outdoor Fabrics
707 N.W. 11th St.
Corvallis, OR 97330
(503) 753-8900
96-in. separating zippers, seam sealer, Thinsulate, Supplex in 65 colors, Versatech, Tactel, Savina DP, Ultrex in 20+ colors, crinkle fabrics. Catalog $1.

Britex Fabrics
146 Geary St.
San Francisco, CA 94108
(415) 392-2910
Microfiber rainwear fabric; swatches $5.

Classic Cloth
34930 U.S. 19 North
Palm Harbor, FL 34684
(800) 237-7739
Vanessa; swatches $5.

Clotilde
1909 S.W. First Ave.
Fort Lauderdale, FL 33315-2100
(800) 772-2891
Sewing notions, Solvy; catalog $2.

G Street Fabrics (Mail-order services)
12240 Wilkins Ave.
Rockville, MD 20852
(301) 231-8960; (800) 333-9191 order line
80-in. separating zippers. Rainwear fabrics; 3-4 free swatches.

handsew, because of their density. It's essential to experiment with your fabrics to obtain the best-looking seams and seam finishes. Happily, I discovered that all the extra topstitching on the ready-to-wear raincoats serves to flatten and finish the seams, compensating for the fact that these fabrics do not press well.

Welts and flat-fell seams are both excellent choices for rainwear, since they both use topstitching to hold them in place. The true welt requires that you trim the under seam allowance away before topstitching, which will produce a more defined seam in some fabrics. For my coat, I chose to use the quicker mock welt seam, which is shown in the top drawing on the facing page. If the fabric ravels, finish the seam allowances with the serger or sewing machine before topstitching. For microfibers, which ravel less than other fabrics, pink the seam allowances to reduce bulk.

To construct the mock welt seam, sew a normal seam right sides together. Press the seam open, then press both seam allowances to one side, using a Teflon press sheet, low heat, and no steam. Serge, zigzag, or pink the edges, then topstitch twice. Try a slightly longer stitch than usual, such as 7 stitches per in., and hold the fabric taut when sewing to avoid puckering. You may not be able to eliminate this problem completely, but I've noticed that even the expensive rainwear has a few puckers.

For my coat, I used the mock welt seam everywhere except the side/underarm seams and the seams that join the collar and collar-stand to the neckline. I even double-topstitched the raglan sleeve seams, ending the stitching in a squared-off box 4½ in. away from the underarm seam, to avoid the curved area.

The more top- and edgestitching you use, the better. Two rows (one on the edge and another ⅜ in. away) will add a finished look to the edges of the fronts, lapels and collar, coat and sleeve hems, the belt and belt loops, wrist straps, fabric guards, and epaulets. For the body hem, add two more rows of stitching 1½ in. away. Make buttonholes on the coat body (keyholes look best, if your machine has that capability).

Install the permanent lining following the guidelines under "Construction" on p. 92, after you've completed the outer shell and the zip-out lining. Then just sew on the buttons, and you're prepared for any weather. ⇨

Cecelia Podolak is a Clothing Specialist with the University of British Columbia and is a frequent contributor to Threads.

Constructing a warm zip-out lining

This easy-to-sew feature converts a raincoat into an all-weather coat. It's a lining sewn to a layer of insulation, with a zipper for easy removal. Sewn completely by machine, it adds a professional ready-to-wear touch.

Pattern adjustments

You will attach the interlining to the lining and treat them as one unit. Both are cut from the lining pattern, with a few minor revisions. The outer edge of this extra layer zips to the coat, and just meets the finished edge of the facing. It needs no seam allowance on the outer edge, which is bound with bias strips before the zipper is added.

Shorten your lining pattern to about 6 in. above the finished length of the coat and add a 2-in. hem. Shorten the sleeve lining to ½ to ⅝ in. above the finished sleeve length, which leaves a 1-in. hem allowance at the lower edge.

Materials

I used Thinsulate, a warm, lightweight microfiber insulation, as interlining in the body of the zip-out lining only; the sleeves are one layer of lining fabric. Other options for the interlining include wool flannels, quilted fabrics, fake fur, polyester fleece, and needle-punch polyester insulation.

You'll need a long separating zipper to run up both front facings and around the neck. Mine ends about 8 in. above the lower edge of the zip-out lining. G Street Fabrics stocks 80-in. No. 3 separating zippers in basic menswear colors, and The Rainshed carries 96-in. ones in tan only (see the sources on p.91). A heavier zipper would add too much bulk. You can shorten zippers from the top end by sewing a bartack at the correct length on each side, cutting ½ in. above the bartack, and folding the ends under. (Remove extra teeth with fine pliers, to reduce bulk. See *Threads* No. 41, p. 16.)

Construction

To construct the zip-out lining, first sew the side seams of the lining and interlining as separate units, and press the seams open. With wrong sides together, join the layers at the outer edges with a serger or zigzag stitch to flatten the bulk. Use the Hong Kong finish (see the bottom drawing on p. 90) to bind the outer edges of the interlining/lining unit with bias strips of self lining.

Next, sew the sleeve underarm seams. To clean finish the hems, serge or zigzag the edge, turn 1 in. under, and machine stitch near the top of the hem. Sew the lining sleeves to the interlining/lining body at the front and back raglan seams.

Turn the body hem to the wrong side and quilt with four rows of machine stitching ⅜ in. apart, as seen in ready-to-wear coats (see the photo at right).

Vent—If your coat has a back vent, make an opening the same height in the back of the zip-out lining, 1½ in. wide, with curved upper corners. Bind the cut edges with bias strips of lining fabric, using the Hong Kong finish.

Zipper—Complete the outer coat, the facing/interfacing unit, the pockets, and any other garment details, but don't insert the permanent lining yet.

Separate the zipper and sew one side under the inner edge of the facing, zipper side up, keeping the teeth about ³/₁₆ in. away from the facing edge, as shown in the drawing on the facing page. Ease the zipper around the curved back-neck facing to avoid stretching the zipper tape. Double-sided basting tape is ideal for holding the zipper while stitching.

Place the second half of the zipper beneath the outer edge of the zip-out lining, allowing the teeth to protrude about ³/₁₆ in. from the edge. Measure and pin to make sure the two halves of the zipper line up. Stitch from the right side of the lining, close to the edge of the bias binding (see the drawing on the facing page).

Permanent lining—After completing the zip-out lining, stitch the assembled permanent lining into the coat. Lap the coat facing over the front and neck edges of the lining, right sides up, matching the stitching lines. Hold the layers in place with double-sided basting tape, if desired. Topstitch through the facing and lining layers from ¾ in. above one hem (leaving room for the lining ease, around the neck, and down to ¾ in. above the other hem, retracing the zipper stitching.

You can finish the lining by hand stitching the sleeve and body hems to the coat, as directed in most pattern guides, but handsewing is difficult in these dense fabrics. To insert the lining completely by machine, try bagging, a technique borrowed from the garment industry. After stitching the hems, the garment is turned right side out through an opening left in the hem or the back vent, then the opening is sewn by hand. Pull the sleeves through the hem opening and stitch. Then sew the hem through the vent opening, and sew one side of the vent. Close the other side of the vent by hand. Read more about this method in my article "Jacket Lining Made Easy" in *Threads* No. 39, pp. 62 to 64.

To prevent the sleeves of the zip-out lining from shifting during wear, anchor them to the underarm seam of the inside coat sleeve with a button on the coat and elastic loop on the lining.—*C.P.*

A close-up look at the removable insulated lining reveals half the zipper hidden under the finished edge of the coat facing, a layer of Thinsulate interlining, the bias-bound edges of the insulated lining, and the hem finished with four rows of channel stitching.

A view of the inner structure of an all-weather coat

The inner layers include a permanent windproof lining and a zip-out insulated lining, for warmth. When the insulated lining is zipped in place, the zipper teeth are hidden.

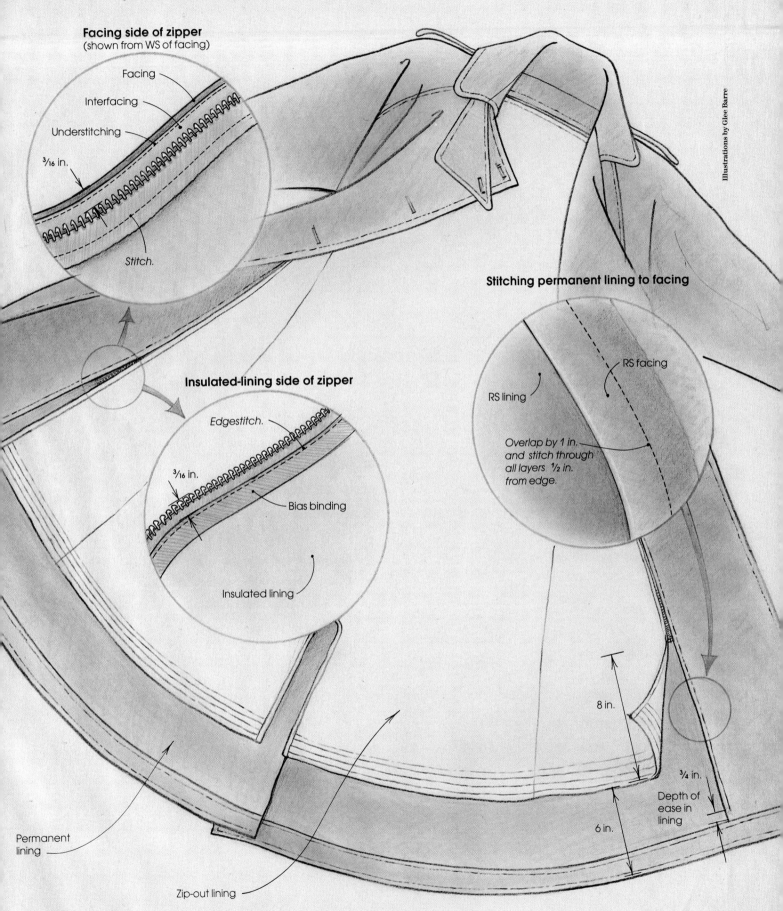

Facing side of zipper
(shown from WS of facing)

Facing

Interfacing

Understitching

3/16 in.

Stitch.

Insulated-lining side of zipper

Edgestitch.

3/16 in.

Bias binding

Insulated lining

Stitching permanent lining to facing

RS facing

RS lining

Overlap by 1 in. and stitch through all layers 1/2 in. from edge.

Permanent lining

Zip-out lining

8 in.

6 in.

3/4 in.

Depth of ease in lining

Illustrations by Glee Barre

Index